SQUARE WATERMELONS

A Journey to Self-Discovery and Life Transformation While Living in Japan (The Japan Chronicles ~ Part I)

MARCUS CHEN

CONTENTS

For Lucas and Sebastian

Prologue

New Year's Eve 1999 — Bondi Beach, Australia

"You've smoked too much weed. There's no way in hell I can fit into this thing," I protested after seeing arms and legs jutting out from the beat-up Toyota station wagon already occupied by eight severely intoxicated Irish men and women.

"C'mon, mate, be a man! It's a short ride to the Opera House and you'll regret for the rest of your life if you missed it," said Connor, a man from Dublin I'd known for only three days and one of my roommates in a cramped hostel room with six bunk beds.

"Alright, you son of a bitch. I'm up for the challenge but I want a seatbelt." I reluctantly accepted the invite.

"You're funny. Now get in because the fireworks won't wait for us," Connor insisted in his thick Irish accent.

My judgment had been severely impaired after too many shots of a cheap vodka that my fellow travelers and I bought from a corner store near the hostel I was staying in. I had much to celebrate.

"Keep your eyes on the road!" Jack shouted at the driver after he barely missed a pedestrian.

"What, mate?" Kelly, with a cigarette in one hand, was bopping his head to the heart-thumping Euro techno as he looked in the rearview mirror.

"Never mind, just get us there safe and sound please," Jack pleaded and quickly followed with, "Where's the joint?"

Kelly, however alert he was, operated the '80s vehicle with gusto and style, racing through the streets of Sydney as if he was doing a stunt on a movie set and no one was riding with him. Inside the discotheque-on-wheels, the eardrum-busting techno, the stench of sweat (it was summertime in Australia), and the smoke from the pot made me nauseous and high at the same time.

"Tonight's either going to be really awesome or it's going to end up very badly," I shouted in Connor's direction.

He shot back, "Mate, you're the luckiest bastard I know and you have the luck of the Irish all around you. Just chill."

In my inebriated state, I mentally replayed the bizarre incident, an emotional rollercoaster that lasted 48 hours the week prior.

A week earlier, Christmas Eve, 1999 — American Consulate in Sydney

⛩

"Hi, I'm an American citizen and I had all my documents stolen. I desperately need a new passport so I can get home in time to attend grad school next week. Please can you help me?" I pleaded to the man who greeted me at the consulate.

"That doesn't sound good. D'you have any paperwork at all? Driver's license, anything?" the junior diplomat inquired.

"No, as I said, I got nothing. No ID, no money, no paperwork. They were stolen from my hostel room in Bondi Beach. I had to borrow money to take a taxi here." Still in shock and very upset, I babbled these words as fast I could.

"Right. What's your name and what are you doing in Sydney?" asked the young man with short, curly blond hair in a navy suit.

"My name's Marcus Chen and I'm from Santa Monica, California, in the U.S. I've been traveling in Europe and Asia in the past few months and I arrived in Sydney two weeks ago," I said very slowly, after having calmed down slightly.

"OK, Marcus, please fill out this form. Make sure you give us your social security number, home address, and any other information you can so that we can confirm your identity."

I wrote down as many personal details as I could and gave them to the stern man who then disappeared for a while. Sitting on an old-fashioned, leather couch for at least half an hour, I thought it was mission impossible to convince them that I was indeed an American. What if they thought I was an undercover intelligence officer or, worse, field ops from Beijing with multiple identities? If I were them, I wouldn't buy that absurd story about some guy traveling around the world for months and ending up in Sydney asking for an American passport, especially if you look East Asian.

What's plan B?

Having no money and no identity papers, I was crumbling inside but I tried as hard as possible to look composed, knowing that at least two cameras were zoomed in on me.

Who do I know in the U.S. government who can prove who I am?

This is really fucked up. I'll never drink again if I get through this ordeal.

Wait, I know Johnny, mayor of Bellflower, CA. Maybe he can help.

How do I get a one-way ticket back to L.A.?

This is hopeless.

I'll mix drinks at a local bar or wait tables, or both, for a while.

No, scratch that, I'll call mom in Manila to wire me U.S.$1,000.

No, I'm too proud to do that. She just gave me $1,000 bucks to buy a new laptop for grad school when I stopped by the Philippines a few weeks earlier. Plus, she'll think I'm a total idiot and disown me.

I'm a disgrace to the family.

How much has the perpetrator already charged on the credit cards he stole from me? $500? $1,000? No, $5,000?

My debt was going up exponentially by the minute.

Am I going to live on the streets of Sydney begging for food until I regain my identity?

I'm in a seriously bad movie. I have big dreams and I need a break to get out of this mess.

Business school starts in a week, halfway across the world in Arizona, and no one knows who I am. Instead of getting my MBA in two years to improve the prospect of having a successful professional career and to do something more meaningful in life, I might have to shovel kangaroo poop in the Sydney zoo for the next 24 months to save enough money to get on a plane to go home.

My life is ruined.

And then, a familiar face appeared.

"Marcus? From Lee High School in San Antonio, Texas?" asked a voice I recognized immediately.

"Holy shit! Russell!" I looked up incredulously and saw a high school classmate I hadn't seen for over ten years. "What the hell are you doing here?" I shot up from the couch and gave the man a big bear hug.

"Nice to see you too. And what the hell are *you* doing, cowboy, in the Land Down Under with that fancy story of being a world traveler and losing your identity?" asked Russell, the guy who in high school drove a pickup truck with a loaded rifle in the cab, now sounding like a law-enforcement officer.

"That's a very long story, Russ, better told over a couple of beers," I responded, still in disbelief, thinking I was seeing a ghost. "I thought you became a consultant in Washington, D.C., with some company called Toilet & Touch?"

"Haha. Close, but no cigar. Deloitte & Touche," Russell corrected me. "I did move to D.C. but management consulting wasn't my kind of rodeo. I ended up joining the Foreign Services and this is my most recent post after spending two years in Angola," he said with a hint of a smile.

"Son of a gun. You're the man!"

"Today's your lucky day, son," Russell continued. "He's good to go," he instructed his junior staff. "We know each other. Let's get him a passport ASAP so he can go home."

A new passport was sorted within the next hour.

I caught up with Russell and gave him the abbreviated version of traveling solo for the past four months across Europe and parts of Asia and ending in Sydney before attending graduate school.

"You're lucky, Marcus. My staff suspected that you're from communist China and trying to infiltrate our great nation," Russell said, halfway joking. "You're not, are you? I mean I haven't seen you in a decade and you speak Mandarin and everything. You didn't go Red on us, did you?" Russell, a former state debate champion in Texas couldn't help himself with the cross-examinations.

"Oh, give me a break, Russ. You know I hate the commies. And besides, the Chinese would have been smart enough to send their spies directly to the U.S," I retorted bluntly. Russell was silent and seemingly waiting for more evidence. "Oh, c'mon, I took this dream trip before business school so I can be more worldly by enriching my knowledge about other cultures, which would then put me in a better position to contribute much more to society. Is that better?"

"Alright, alright, I'm only joking and I believe you. I always knew you were destined for greatness. I'll be following you through grad school and your career later on to see how things turn out. Listen, why don't you join me for a New Year's party with some Norwegian and Swedish diplomats in a couple of days by the harbor?"

"Would be rude not to." I gladly agreed to it. "And by the way, I think you might have just saved me from having my life destroyed."

"Take it easy, kid. It's what friends do and I'm just doing my job. Just make sure you do your thing to help others in need in the future."

It was a most bizarre and satisfying way to run into an old friend a world away. Sadly, after that mini-reunion with Russ in Sydney for a couple of days, I hadn't seen him since and I heard later that he was posted in East Timor a year later.

⛩

That afternoon, just when I thought things couldn't possibly get any better, I got a call back at the hostel from the Bondi Beach police station.

"Sir, someone's turned in a stolen wallet and passport, still with $1,000 cash stashed inside the passport holder. We think this could be yours. Why don't you come into the station?"

"Are you kidding me? The money's still there? And the plane ticket?" I questioned the only man at the station that afternoon when I arrived there.

"Yep, you look like the man in your driver's license picture. I'm afraid there's no more cash in your wallet and your credit cards are gone unfortunately."

"Wow! How did this end up here?" I asked the police officer.

"Someone from the hostel chased down this bloke who was running down the street with your stuff and the guy dropped these items as he ran. You're very fortunate the $1,000 is still here."

"Holy smokes. Thank you! Thank you! Thank you! This is the only money I have in my life at this point and it's from my mom. It's a long story," I said to the kind officer.

I offered the man a $100 note to thank him but he respectfully refused so I gave him a big hug instead.

I had gone from "This is the worst day in my life" to "This is a Christmas miracle" in less than 48 hours.

⛩

The second miracle in as many days was that the nine of us in that rickety station wagon somehow managed to arrive without a scratch at the Opera House just before midnight. We were just in time to witness the most spectacular pyrotechnics in front of the iconic building.

"Told you we'd get here fine. You owe me one," Connor said with a smirk.

"I do; more than one I think," I replied as the explosion of the fireworks began to light up the skies around this amazingly beautiful city surrounded by water. The stress, fatigue, and anxiety that I'd experienced on the way to the harbor quickly dissipated and were replaced with joy and wonder. I had goosebumps all over.

"Behold the world-famous Sydney Opera House. Shall we have a Red Bull Vodka to commemorate this occasion?" I offered Connor after a rush of adrenaline from admiring the perfectly choreographed explosion of fireworks as we joined thousands of other revelers from around the world.

"Couldn't think of a better way to usher in the new millennium." Connor gladly accepted.

We managed to find the concoction to toast to the once-in-a-millennium event and I found myself hugging and kissing generously the strangers around us. I had no recollection of how we got back to Bondi Beach later that morning but I do remember crashing a party at some bar by the beach.

"Hey, man, is this the most amazing evening of your life or what? Your shirt smells like beer, pot, and perfume, and you have lipstick on your shirt collar," Connor commented and chuckled at the same time.

"One of the best for sure. Glad you dragged me into the Irish limo of death, you crazy leprechaun."

"C'mon, mate, life doesn't get any better. We got the number one DJ in the world playing on Bondi, beautiful half-naked girls all over, no Y2K catastrophe, what else can you ask for?" Connor paused for a second then out of the blue added, "So you still wanna go back to L.A.? You should just hang out here with us, take a year off before grad school. Life's too short," Said the Dubliner who planned to be in Sydney for a year to work as an IT professional.

"It's very tempting. But I have big plans for life and I'm out of money, bro. This was my once-in-a-life time trip before things get serious and I need to get a real job then buy a house and have a family, etc. It's been incredibly fun and eye-opening these past few months but I have obligations and the show has to end." I was barely awake at that time and had downgraded to drinking some Victoria Bitter.

"You're way too serious. Lighten up, Yankee. You'll never live and travel like this again, trust me on this one. And by the way, you're only young and free once."

And with those words of wisdom, Connor stumbled and disappeared into the darkness and it was the last time I ever saw him.

I took a stroll down the beach, exhausted from the celebrations to welcome Y2K and all the drama and activities in and around Bondi Beach and Sydney in the three weeks prior. I found an empty spot and sat on the soft, golden sand at the crescent-shaped beach to appreciate the color of the sky morphing from black to various shades of gray, indigo, and finally into a light blue. It was the first sunrise of the new millennium.

Being single in my 20s with an excellent job and living a kilometer from the Pacific Ocean was an amazing life in retrospect. I'd been blessed to have worked for a Fortune 500 company already and had lived in the perfect-weather Santa Monica with its endless beach, something I still miss to this day. But somehow, I'd felt life could be much more meaningful and I'd decided to go back to school to expand my horizons and be in a better position to pursue other worthy causes. After being accepted to the grad school of my choice, I'd resigned from my job and liquidated my life savings so I could travel the world for a few months. The decision to leave my job early to travel was the right one, but if I could go back in time to coach my former self, I would have set aside an amount of money in the bank as being penniless is just about the worst feeling I've ever experienced in life.

Young, idealistic, and full of energy, I was also very naïve in so many ways as the trip that started with a one-way ticket to Paris had almost ended up in a total disaster in Sydney. With some inexplicable luck, the journey-of-a-lifetime in 1999-2000 that took me to 15 countries across Europe, Southeast Asia, Australia, and New Zealand turned out just about perfect in the end. It was truly eye-opening throughout the four months and it played a huge role in shaping my mindset, life goals, and professional aspirations. It became the catalyst for my choosing a career which allowed me to venture to even more parts of the world and led me eventually to Japan on an expat assignment.

It was the beginning of a passage that led me to live a vastly different life than the one I'd imagined before I took the trip. The experience, insights, and lessons from that life-altering journey were easily worth more than ten times the investment as they propelled me to set the goal of becoming a global marketing executive. After graduate school, working abroad was always in the plan. The destination, however, was a bit of an accident.

I'd studied six languages (Spanish, French, German, Tagalog, Latin, and Mandarin) and I thought surely, I would be able to go to a country where I knew the language and the culture well. Life is dynamic and things didn't quite turn out as planned.

I ended up in a place known for sashimi, *manga* (comics), karaoke, and, as I discovered later, bizarre, square watermelons.

Episode 1 (Ichi): The Accidental Gaijin

Eight years later. Fall, 2008 — New Jersey, USA

"Hello, Marcus. This is Toshi calling from Tokyo. Do you have a few minutes now?" asked the gentleman who'd just rung my office phone. I immediately knew who he was.

"Hi, Yamamoto-san, great to hear from you. Of course. Now's perfect," I responded nervously.

"I've reviewed your credentials thoroughly and I think you can definitely contribute a lot to our global marketing team. I would like to offer you the opportunity to work in the global home office in Japan for three years. What do you think?" asked Yamamoto-san, who asked Westerners to call him Toshi. He was the vice president of the global marketing department.

"I love it. I accept. Thank you very much for the opportunity, sir. I can't wait to join the team," I said, barely able to contain my excitement.

And so, it happened. Eight years after Sydney, and having set a goal to become an expat, I was given the chance to experience working and living abroad with a top 20 global pharmaceutical company in a country I'd admired greatly but had never been to.

After hearing all kinds of incredible stories and fantasizing about being an expat, it was now my turn to put my education and training to work and to live this privileged life of experiencing exotic corners of the world. It was hard to believe that with my very humble beginnings as the son of an immigrant, armed only with a big dream to succeed in life but with minimal direction, I was now blessed with this unbelievable opportunity. I pumped my fist in the air a few times in my cubicle and went for a walk along the little creek by the office to digest what had just happened.

My master plan at Thunderbird, the business school I'd gone to, was to secure a job with a large global company that would value my global mindset and language skills and send me abroad. This job happened quite a few years behind plan but it was better late than never. It was a goal I'd set in my 20s so I didn't really think through how such a choice would affect my career and my personal life since I wasn't quite done growing up.

I'd done well academically in business school, made lots of friends, and had a tremendous amount of fun. I'd also incurred a sizable debt despite receiving nearly a full scholarship. I wasn't worried as I was confident I would soon be gainfully employed with a reputable company and my student loans would go away quickly. The only problem was that there'd been no full-time job offer of any kind for me at graduation and my world had come crashing down suddenly. I blamed everyone and everything — the economy and the September 11th attack on the World Trade Center in New York that year. I'd been unemployed, had severe depression, lived off my credit card, and tried to take life one day at a time, far from the plan I'd envisioned. It'd been the darkest period of my life and I wish now that I could tell my younger self then that it was only a test and that everything would be fine in the end.

Hope and faith had helped me to crawl out from the abyss eventually. I'd found my way into sales in the pharmaceutical industry, working my way up to marketing a few years later. And then, I was handed this break of a lifetime — the opportunity to work in Tokyo.

⛩

I returned to the good news at hand and thought I needed to share it with my wife, Renee. The only challenge was that I'd made up my mind to take the job despite the imperfect timing. Renee had just started the first year of law school in New York.

How would I break the news? The timing was horrible. This wasn't fair for Renee.

On three occasions we'd lived in different cities for months at a time and managed to keep our relationship intact. This time the distance was 11,000 kilometers and we would be in two different continents.

What do I do if she doesn't support it? The prospect of having to decline the offer later was hard to accept after I'd worked so hard. At the same time, I was conflicted with doing something that might go against Renee's wishes.

"Hey, guess what? I've been offered a three-year assignment in Tokyo!" I said, my heart racing.

"What? Shut up!"

"Yeah, I just got a verbal offer from the main guy in Tokyo to join the global marketing team in Japan as an expat." I toned down the enthusiasm a bit as I hadn't discussed the topic with my other half of the family. I expected her reaction to be neutral to negative.

"Wow! That's awesome!" Renee was in the middle of preparing for a contract law exam and I had caught her by surprise.

"It's amazing. The duration is longer than what I expected but I think I should take it." I felt guilty saying this but I spoke my mind.

There was a long silence on the other end. I thought she must be pissed off and preparing to talk me out of it. The pause was killing me.

Forget about it. This would never work, I thought.

"Well, I know it's something you've really wanted for a while," Renee finally spoke up.

"Yes, it is." Surprised, I was waiting for the big blow.

Another long pause.

"I know the timing's awful," I said, still waiting for the verdict.

"I'm happy and excited for you. But it won't work for me because I just started law school."

More silence.

What will the future attorney say next?

"But I think you should take it. I mean, after all that you went through since graduating from business school and to get this position now. This job offer's a small miracle and you'd be an idiot if you didn't accept it," she said.

It was going much better than I expected.

"I'm glad you're supportive. I think being an expat will build my character, expand my worldview, and, you know, help make me a more valuable contributor to the company and overall be good for my career. The timing's never perfect with these things," I replied, having rehearsed it in my head just in case I got a major push-back.

"It's fine. We'll have to live in two countries for a while. It won't be the first time we live apart from each other and I want you to live your dream," Renee responded. She'd twice followed me to a different state in the U.S. because of work and she'd built a system to deal with the transition.

Still feeling guilty and a bit selfish, I asked, "Are you sure you're OK with this?"

"Just do it already. You went from being unemployed with a huge debt to somehow finding your way back to becoming a marketer in the drug industry. Now you have this amazing, once-in-a-career opportunity. Don't be stupid!" Renee said firmly, almost upset.

"You're right. I don't know if I'll get a chance like this again." A perfectionist at heart, I questioned the timing but knew it was the right decision.

"Remember those months when you were a test-car driver in the Arizona desert for Chrysler, doing the graveyard shift, having no sleep, and not knowing when you'd have a 'real' job again?" Renee reminded me of the time when I was just 'hanging out,' financed by credit card companies and not knowing where I might be the next month.

"How could I forget? I took on more debt so that I could stay at a cheap motel that I couldn't afford, living one day at a time and feeling sorry for myself." I remembered well those character-building days when my confidence level was rock bottom and the future was obscure.

"You said to me that it was all temporary and it was just a matter of time before you accomplished your goal of becoming a global marketer." Renee reminded me of something I'd almost forgotten.

Before I could reply, she continued with the pep talk. "And you went from the bottom of the heap in your sales territory to becoming the top dog in the country, even though you hated some of your managers."

"Yeah, because I really wanted to get into marketing and I did my very best in sales."

"Well, it helped, didn't it? You said it yourself that you must always do your very best at the current job while not losing sight of the prize. You got into marketing, you kicked ass, and now you got offered this fantasy job. I don't know why you're even hesitating."

I realized that not only should I do this, but I *must* do it.

"OK, let's do this!" I said finally.

Renee was extremely generous with her support of my assignment, as she had been the previous times when we were living apart in the name of my career progression. That night we went to a sushi restaurant nearby to celebrate the momentous occasion.

Early January 2009 — Tokyo, Japan

"Where am I?" I asked myself for the first few days when I woke up in the morning.

I would confirm my whereabouts by looking out the master bedroom window at the gorgeous view of the snow-capped Mt. Fuji.

"Holy crap. I'm not in New Jersey anymore." Every morning it was the same startled reaction.

It took about a week before the reality of having begun a new life in a land 11,000 kilometers away really set in. I felt like an adolescent again, as if experiencing living abroad for the first time, full of curiosity and anticipation. Japan would be the seventh country in which I'd spent at least three months but I was just as excited as the first time I arrived in a foreign country when I was ten. Japan hadn't been anywhere near the top of the list of countries I thought I would work in. I'd imagined, and would have preferred, France, Spain, Germany, somewhere in Latin America, or greater China, countries I'd lived or studied the language. But there I was, in Japan, a country that was so close to where I was born, yet so far away from what I knew and where I grew up in America.

It was an exhilarating feeling. How lucky I was to go from unemployment to expat assignment in a span of a few years.

I'd become an accidental *gaijin* (foreigner) and I was ready for my adventure to begin.

Episode 2 (Ni): Speed-Eating Contest

"Iow was your first day at work in the new office?" Renee asked.

"I think I'm screwed," I said.

"That good, huh? What happened?"

"Well, I work in an office where no one talks to each other. Nobody goes to lunch unless the bell rings. My boss sits right next to me and prefers sending emails instead of just speaking to me. I might have to start smoking if I want to go anywhere in this company as everyone seems to. It's gonna be a long three years."

"Holy crap. That doesn't sound good."

Earlier that day I'd been greeted by Ono-san, whom I'd met several times from earlier projects in the company. "Welcome, Chen-san. We have been waiting for you." Ono-san, whose job responsibility was a bit obscure, came down to the reception area to formally welcome me to the team on my first official day in the office.

"*Ohayō gozaimasu* (Good morning), *Ono-san*. I'm very excited to be here," I said with a slight bow.

"Hi. OK, nice to see you, Chen-san. Let me start by telling you about this neighborhood. Nihonbashi is a historical area and one of the oldest parts of Tokyo and home to several of the largest Japan-based pharmaceutical companies. This district is so important for the drug industry in Japan that it has its own Medicine God and shrine. Every August there is a festival to celebrate the Medicine God who protects and ensures the prosperity of these drug companies, including ours." Ono-san was very enthusiastic as he described the area while we took the elevator to our floor.

"Cool and interesting. So, could you please show me my office?" I was eager to get settled and start a new chapter.

"Well, Chen-san, you don't really have an office but we all have our own desk, including Brewer-san." Ono-san, an alumnus of Tokyo University, considered Japan's top academic institution, reminded me that there would be little privacy at work.

"No problem, I knew that already; it's just habit. Can you also introduce me to some other team members in our group?"

For the first half hour or so, I nodded my head a lot and said *"Hajimemashite"* (Nice to meet you) to lots of people. Everyone stood up from their chairs, bowed, and shook my hand as I approached them. They were the folks in this prestigious department called International Business and Global Marketing, which was the envy of many in the organization.

"And this is your desk, right next to Brewer-san. He is just at the lounge and will be right back." Ono-san went around the row of desks that faced each other and sat down right in front of me on the other side.

Although I knew about the open-floor seating, I did get a little depressed after seeing my desk. Back in the U.S., my office space was about four times the size of this and with a door and walls. This desk was about 120 centimeters wide and 60 centimeters deep. Small and uninspiring, although functional. A pile of stationery and log-in instructions to my PC were already placed on my desk. There was a tiny bit of separation, in the form of a 15-centimeter-tall metal divider, between the people that sat across from me and me. However, it didn't prevent me from smelling the cigarette breath and seeing stained and crooked yellow teeth from my new colleagues. Everyone was busy typing away, on the keyboard or on their smartphone, or both. After five minutes of uncomfortable silence, I decided to look for the boss.

"When you said 'lounge,' do you mean the smoking lounge?" I asked Ono-san to clarify, hoping to find Brewer-san, a guy called Ian whom I already knew, so I could say hello and find out what I should do for the rest of the week.

"Yes, yes, sorry, it's around the corner. There you can get free coffee and tea. Please help yourself." Ono-san politely pointed in the direction of my new boss and went back to his world of fixating his eyeballs on his computer monitor.

Like most traditional Japanese offices, the open-floor layout meant everybody saw each other. A department VP sat behind a desk, the same size as the others, and faced, at a right-angle, a row of desks filled with his subordinates who sat across from each other underneath rows of fluorescent lights. The desk closest to the VP was the highest-ranking employee and the one farthest away the lowest person in the totem pole. In a company of more than 10,000 people, only about a dozen or so employees had an actual office with a door at HQ. I was so used to having an office in the U.S. and having only a desk felt uncomfortable.

"There you are! Must be where all the important people hang out." I found Ian and waved and spoke through the glass divider but he didn't seem to hear me. I hit the 'green tea' button on the coffee and tea dispenser, got myself a cup of instant tea, and went inside the 'lounge.'

How fitting that the first sighting in Japan of Ian, the Englishman from Manchester and the first *gaijin* to come to the Japan home office some ten years prior for an assignment and stayed for good, was in the smoking lounge. The image I have in mind of Ian from previous meetings in Europe and America was that he almost always had a cigarette in hand, or a glass or Burgundy, or both.

"Welcome to the jungle. We've been looking forward to having you here. But first, let me finish getting some fresh air," he joked. Ian quickly introduced me to a couple of other people who were with him in the lounge while I tried desperately not to suffocate from the dense tobacco fog.

"You know, this where it all happens, right here. And if you don't smoke, you may want to consider it. Cigarettes are so cheap here, it's nearly compulsory to take up the habit," Ian said, half joking, and let out another big puff.

Ian was referring to how important discussions often took place in the lounge but more often, they happened after hours in *nomikai* (drinking parties), one of which was planned in my honor the very first night I was in the office.

"I think I'll stick with alcohol and green tea for now," I said as I took another sip of the free, but otherwise disgusting, green liquid from a very dated machine.

In Japan at the time, more than 40 percent of the population smoked cigarettes and it was still quite common in the workplace. For about $4.00 you could choose between a Starbucks coffee and a pack of Seven Stars; many chose the latter.

"Did Ono-san introduce you to everyone?" Ian asked.

"I think so, but I don't feel very welcome here. Should I be worried?"

"No one's going to talk to you in the office for at least a week. But don't worry, they're all just curious and a little shy. You'll get lots of questions tonight at the *nomikai* after everyone's had a few drinks," Ian said as he finished his smoke.

After my initial introductions that first day to some colleagues on the floor, it would take several more days for them to work up the courage to speak to *gaijin* number two. Virtually everyone understood and spoke excellent English as most had studied or worked overseas or both. Some even spoke Mandarin Chinese and Spanish because of their business dealings with affiliate offices.

There were a few female colleagues although no one could recall ever seeing a lady sitting at a VP's desk at this very old-fashioned, century-old company. I would learn later that most women wouldn't return to work after they had children. Many chose not to come back or were strongly "encouraged" to take care of their family at home.

There were about a hundred Japanese suits packed into this one floor where my phone line was shared by at least a dozen other people in my section. There were no personal voicemails because we were supposed to take messages for each other. On a floor the size of a supermarket and with this many people, I thought it would be like working in a New York Stock Exchange trading floor where it would be noisy and chaotic. On the contrary, the silence was deafening.

"It's awfully quiet here, Ian. Is it usually like this in this office?" I asked.

"Well, it's polite not to be too loud. We can always book a meeting room if we need to discuss something," Ian spoke softly, sitting just a meter from me.

Seriously? Book a meeting room just to talk? I didn't sign up for this! I thought and nearly said it out loud but held back.

Based on what I'd experienced so far that first day, I thought I would probably develop clinical depression, speech impairment, and lung cancer during my assignment.

I'm so screwed!

And so, I found myself whispering to my boss, trying to fit in and not disturb the quiet harmony on the floor. Although English in origin, I figured Ian had been there for so long that he'd probably adopted much of the Japanese ways of doing things. It was my first day so I held in my irritation that I had to email someone sitting so close to me and instead I exchanged a few emails with him while waiting for lunch to come.

After trying the equally horrible instant coffee, I had a "crash onboarding" of the company and the department with our team administrative assistant, Yoko-san, who was very pleasant and it helped to make time pass more quickly. But I looked at my watch and it was barely 10:30 a.m.

I'll never make it in this place.

"So, Ian, you feel like grabbing some lunch today?" I was hoping to get more scoop about the people in the office and how things worked there.

"Thanks, I think I'll pass. I'm not big on lunch but I think you should try to know your new colleagues. Just about everyone eats lunch in the canteen downstairs and it's very cheap."

"What's good down there?" I asked.

"I don't know. I've never eaten down there since I came here almost ten years ago. I think nothing's horrible," Ian said.

"Sounds reassuring," I said, not sure what Ian's comment meant.

"By the way, don't be offended if they eat super-fast and don't talk to you. Eating to most Japanese is more of a functional activity to feed the body, not really for enjoyment or relaxation," he added.

"Great. Thanks for the warning. Maybe I'll join you for coffee afterwards. Where will you be?"

"It won't be difficult to find me. Try one of the cafés nearby that allow smoking," he said with a slight grin.

Soon a bell rang, indicating lunchtime, and everyone left their desk in unison to head down to the bunker of the building.

Am I in a middle school or something?

I followed after them and watched my colleagues order and devour their *ramen* (wheat noodles), *soba* (buckwheat noodles), or *gohan* (a rice bowl dish) with curry in about five minutes and without speaking a word to anyone next to them.

OK, maybe I, *gaijin* number two, was too intimidating for them and made them uncomfortable. I looked at my bowl. I still had half of my noodles and I consider myself a very fast eater.

After the speed-eating contest, which reminded me of the annual Nathan's Hot Dog Eating Contest in the U.S. where a Japanese man name Kobayashi had won several times, they hurried back up to their desks to do nothing.

After the first couple of days of watching this eating competition at lunch, I started to play a game to see who would win at lunch.

Will it be Ono-san, who hails from Osaka and slurps the loudest?

Will it be Tanaka-san, who grew up in Shikoku and speaks as fast as he sucks down the rice bowl?

Or could it be Honda-san, a proud Sendai native who spent time in California, who doesn't seem to breathe when he inhales his food?

It was always very close because even at lunch, they tried to finish the task at the same time. What a conformist society!

I struggled to make conversations during lunch, even after weeks of intaking food with them, and gave up altogether in favor of going for a stroll in nearby stores. I discovered serendipitously a nice book store called Maruzen which stocked a decent selection of English books. It became a daily routine for some weeks where I sought refuge and sanity.

I did find Ian on the first attempt at a very smoky café. He sat right by the glass wall looking down at his *Herald Tribune* crossword puzzle, deep in thought with a pencil in one hand and a Marlboro Light in the other. I stood right in front of him for two seconds and waved on the other side of the glass. He didn't move and I left the man alone.

At 5:30 p.m. a bell rang again, this time indicating that it was time to go home. The second bell was highly symbolic as nobody moved at 5:30 (except for Ian and me) and most chose to stay until 7 or 8 p.m. with a few die-hards staying until 9 or 10. The rule of thumb is that one should leave only after the department head has left. Everyone is an actor or an obedient soldier or both.

Episode 3 (San): Orientation

"*Ohayō gozaimasu, Chen-san.* Saito-san is here for you," Imaizumi-san, the head concierge, said over the intercom and woke both of us up Saturday morning.

"For real? It's like super early. And who's Saito?" Renee asked, having just flown over to visit me.

"Yeah, I forgot to tell you. The company booked us an expert guide to take us around and show us the neighborhood a bit to get us oriented."

"We don't need that; everything's on the internet." Still jetlagged, Renee was sleepy and irritated.

After throwing on some clothes and sneakers, we went down to meet this retired professor turned tour guide, Saito-san.

"Good morning. You must be Chen-san. I'm Mr. Saito." Saito-san stood up from a chair in the lobby, dressed very formally in a suit, with a hat, a map of the neighborhood, and a picture of me.

"*Ohayō gozaimasu,* Saito-san. This is my wife, Renee. Thanks for coming on a Saturday morning. Can we please go to Starbucks before we go on the tour?" I desperately needed caffeine.

"We're in Japan. We should go anywhere but Starbucks," Saito-san replied.

"OK, any place is fine. Maybe we can start walking to that Tokyo Midtown place. There must be a coffee shop there."

We stumbled out of our apartment and headed toward Tokyo Midtown, a fairly new development with large office buildings, upscale residences, a shopping mall, a Ritz-Carlton Hotel, and a beautiful Japanese garden.

"What's this thing to the right? Some temple?" Renee asked Saito-san as we walked past a group of older folks doing tai chi in slow motion in front of an ancient-looking stone and wooden structure.

"It's actually a 400-year-old shrine," Saito-san said. "Very famous. Good for praying for babies."

"OK, and what's this large, walled-off complex to the left? Looks important," Renee continued, slowly waking up.

"That's the American Embassy living quarters. It's where the diplomats and their families who work at the embassy are housed. About 1,000 Americans live inside the compound," I said before Saito-san could get to it. I'd learned about it during my apartment-hunting trip a couple of months prior.

"So, you moved halfway across the world just to be next door to home? What's wrong with you?" Renee quipped.

"It's a strategic move. You know if the shit goes down with anti-American sentiments, and there are still some, we're a stone's throw away from safety. Trust me on this one, I think about these scenarios." I said that probably a bit too loudly, although only half joking, but Saito-san heard me well.

"Well, the war was over more than 60 years ago now. It would never happen again after the two atomic bombs from America and where millions of Japanese people died. We rewrote the constitution to prohibit an active military force," the professor said solemnly, sounding like a historian.

"I'm very sorry, Saito-san. We should talk about something different and more important, like finding some nice pastry and good coffee." I was focused on the task at hand.

After getting some croissants and caffeine from Maison de Kayser and feeling human again, we let Saito-san take us on his pre-planned tour.

"So, first of all, Akasaka, where we are, means Red Hill in Japanese. It's known for its many government buildings and embassies, including the American Embassy and its living quarters, which is right next to your building as you already know. Akasaka is in a district or mini-city called Minato-Ku, one of the 22 'wards' in greater Tokyo. It's very much the heart of Tokyo and where many expats choose to live because many people who work and live there speak English and many businesses cater to the foreigners."

The professor, sounding like an experienced guide who's memorized his speech, went on a five-minute monologue, seemingly in one single breath, to describe a bit more about the history of the Red Hill. I wanted to interrupt and tell him that I already knew all that but felt it would be impolite.

"Yes, it's why we chose this apartment because it's very central and easy for me to get to work," I responded. "So, we're already familiar with the main stores and subway stations and all that. Maybe we can finish the orientation earlier?" I asked after we'd walked for at least three kilometers by 10 a.m.

It was a Saturday morning in a mostly business district so the streets were quiet except for a few elderly couples out on a morning stroll, over-dressed for what I considered a mild winter's day but cold by Tokyo standard. A few stray cats roamed the alleyways looking for breakfast and occasionally we heard the "ding" of a bell from bikes that Japanese ladies pedaled to and from the closest grocery store. We smelled the incense from a small temple as we walked by after worshippers had said their prayers.

Comparing this to a big American city like New York City where skyscrapers dominate the skyline and where cars are abundant and most streets are wide, very small alleyways permeate through the Tokyo cityscape with mostly unattractive, blocky concrete buildings that are modern but seem to lack character. Many of these homes or high rises were built very quickly after WWII when the U.S. military decimated the city with firebombs. As land is scarce in Japan, many of these buildings look cramped next to each other and appear much skinnier than their Western counterparts.

We strolled past a couple of small, wooden houses that had dozens of potted bonsai plants in a small yard that looked to have survived the ravages of war and stood in stark contrast to the much more modern homes and buildings. The narrow roads, easier to navigate on foot or bikes, seemed to have been there for centuries and were simply paved over with asphalt during the industrial revolution in the early 20th century.

The streets were impeccably clean in a city where public trash cans were hard to find. We passed a few more early risers on our orientation tour and tried to make eye contact but no one acknowledged us.

Saito-san was relentlessly thorough and determined to show us everything that was on his to-do list. Typical of many Japanese, he was following orders and wasn't about to deviate from his instructions. The professor was a bit irritated when I proposed an early end to our tour and he insisted he must finish the job.

"OK, maybe just a couple more places as we've already looked up most of the items on the venues of interest on your list," I pleaded with the man, our stomachs growling and eyelids struggling to stay open.

"And this is the famous hill that was featured in a Japanese TV show, and then this famous shrine is where a famous general committed *harakiri* (Japanese ritual suicide with samurai sword) to show his loyalty to Emperor Meiji when the ruler died."

What the? Seriously?

Saito-san continued his memorized lines while Renee and I mentally checked out after four hours of this long march with no food or water. I was ready to do the *harakiri* myself.

I appreciated his enthusiasm but I didn't care much about some sitcom I'd never heard of and even less about the sacrificial place where a famous general plunged a samurai sword into his abdomen.

After thanking him for his time and insisting we had gotten all we needed, we celebrated by eating a big bowl of *katsudon* (pork cutlet rice bowl) and then passed out in our mansion by 1 p.m.

Episode 4 (Shi): Losing my Religion

I f moving is a royal pain in general, moving to a foreign country where you don't speak the language and having to furnish an apartment and make it into a livable home is a massive undertaking. The mission the next day was to fill this empty flat with household essentials such as eating utensils, small appliances, etc. A colleague had recommended that we go to Yodobashi Camera, an electronics superstore in Akihabara, which is known for being the mecca of electronics and for the maid cafés where ladies dressed in a French maid costume provide a range of services from haircuts to serving drinks.

We managed to find this mega camera shop where my colleague had insisted I could find everything I needed. I was quite skeptical. When we arrived at the twelve-story building, we almost immediately turned around and left as young women who looked like spaceship flight attendants greeted us.

"What the hell?" It was all Renee could say as we stared at the young ladies in their skintight, white tops; very short, white mini-skirts; white knee-high boots; and futuristic-looking white hats.

"Um, let's give it a chance. I see some appliances back there."

"I'm sure you do. But why are they talking like little girls in grade school? It's very annoying," Renee asked as the women spoke in a high-pitched voice into handheld microphones to promote items on sale.

"I think it's cultural. I believe some men find this to be attractive. You know, the sound of young girls." I'd read that somewhere.

"So this country is full of pedophiles or tolerate them? Great! So glad I came!"

"Well let's just find what we need and get out. Sound like a plan?"

Bizarre as it might seem, we quickly realized that you could also pick up a Rolex and get a bespoke suit made while buying a PlayStation 3. The top floor is dedicated to restaurants, typical of most department stores in Japan, allowing shoppers to take a break and spend more money. It was Best Buy meets Costco on steroids and all in one giant box.

After the initial shock factor, we spent an entire day there and purchased many essential items including a vacuum cleaner, a flat-screen TV, a rice cooker, a hot water machine (essential in Japan), a PlayStation that doubled as a DVD player, and a bunch of cleaning agents. Thanks to a generous move-in allowance from my employer, we were liberal with our pickings and enjoyed the shopping experience, hectic as it was. With rental furniture being delivered the day earlier, the apartment was becoming fully functional.

The next day, I got a surprise visit.

"Chen-san, New York Yankees article. I bring this for you." My landlord, a serious fan of the celebrated baseball team from New York, made a point of coming to meet his new *gaijin* tenant.

"*Arigatō gozaimasu* (Thank you), Watanabe-san. I'm not from New York but just across the river, in New Jersey," I replied.

"Ah, no problem. The same! But Yankees are the best! Hideki Matsui, the Godzilla, is *ichiban ne* (number one, right)?" The 152-centimeter-tall man in a dark gray suit enthused about the Yankees and said quite a few more things I couldn't understand.

"Yes, Matsui, a very good player with many home runs. And your mansion is in a great location. I love it here." I complimented the sharply-dressed older gentleman for having good taste in his investment in the fancy flat; what Tokyoites called "mansions."

"*Ii des ne* (It's good, right)? Very convenient. You can visit the Imperial Palace and Gardens, only two kilometers away. The Diet building, also walking distance. Many subway stations and places to eat and shop. The view of Fuji-san, a special present for you." The man who has made his fortune building golf courses in Japan described his mansion with pride.

"Yes, I already know; it's why I chose your mansion. Thank you again for the Yankees article." I was trying to end the conversation and get back to unpacking.

"You know the Mitsubishi Corporation made this building, only six months old. And you are my first tenant. I put very nice appliances, Miele washer and dryer from Germany and also the Mitsubishi refrigerator. And tomorrow I bring you microwave oven because I know Americans must have a microwave."

I let the recently retired man continue, having already familiarized myself with every piece of equipment in the flat.

"Everything has electronic control, from your bathtub to your toilet, security cameras, lights in every room, and of course air conditioning. Very modern, easy, and perfect for young people like you. You also have a beautiful veranda to see the city, parking space for a car in the garage, two bicycle parking spaces, and a temperature-controlled trunk room for storage, all in the basement."

The man simply couldn't stop talking up his place that I'd already committed to living in for three years. I just wanted to have another shot of coffee and unpack.

"Yes, Watanabe-san, I love everything here, especially the talking bathtub and the toilet with a spray and blow dryer. It's the nicest place I've ever lived in my life." I threw out more signals to send the man back to his golf course.

I'd gone from living in a modest townhome in a working-class neighborhood in Jersey to one of the poshest areas of Tokyo overnight and I felt completely out of place. This wasn't my scene as I was (still am) just a simple person with super-humble beginnings.

This high-end mansion, which would have cost $1.6 Million in 2009 to purchase, was still the fanciest place I've ever lived in to this date.

"OK, Chen-san, if you need anything, please tell Imaizumi-san downstairs. He is my friend and he will take care of you. Don't worry." And with that, he bowed deeply and said his good-bye.

A minute later I looked down to the surface street and saw Watanabe-san's chauffeur dashing out of his black Lexus sedan to open the door for him. Imaizumi-san quickly followed just a few steps behind, stopped beside the car to bow about 45 degrees, and stayed down until the car disappeared from his view.

This stuff was getting real.

⛩

"*Irasshaimase* (Welcome)!" shouted a man with a headband, who looked like a chef, behind a counter as soon as Renee and I walked into Kunpu restaurant in Roppongi.

"*Konban wa* (Good evening)," I said to the lady at the entrance.

"*Futari* (Two people)?" she asked.

"*San-nin desu, tomodachi to issho ni* (Three persons, friends, together)," I managed to explain in my rudimentary Japanese. Six months of self-study with *Rosetta Stone* before arriving in Tokyo was at least good enough for dining out.

"*Ah, Asakawa-san no yoyaku* (Mr. Asakawa's reservation)?" asked the lady, dressed in a basic, traditional Japanese kimono.

"*Sō desu* (Yes)," I replied.

"*Kochira e. Dōzo.* (This way. Please.)" She led us to a semi-private booth around the corner.

"There you are, Marcus, so good to see you." Taka, an investment banker, stood up from his seat and squeezed my hand firmly.

"You look exactly the same, my friend," I told him.

"You too. Are you ready for your new adventure?"

I'd read about *izakaya*, which are traditional Japanese pubs, but it was my first time visiting one. Patrons typically have to remove their shoes and sit on a *tatami* (straw mat) on the floor. This one was no different. I'd bought new socks immediately before moving to Japan as I knew I would be showcasing them frequently in social outings. Servers in these *izakaya* are dressed in traditional kimonos and walk on sandals, reflecting a tradition that has been passed down from many generations ago.

One of the greatest joys in life is meeting up with old friends in another place far away, especially after a long time of not seeing each other. In this case, eight years had gone by since I saw my former business-school classmate Takayuki, who goes by Taka, a Japanese national and a captain of his industry. Our lives had dramatically changed to say the least. We were no longer poor (thank God!) and we'd done some interesting things after the grueling business-school curriculum (OK, there was heavy partying too!). Taka had gone on to work for several large global investment banks and had done quite well. I'd told him I was moving to Tokyo and he'd invited Renee and me to have dinner at a traditional Japanese *izakaya* near our mansion.

"I'm pumped. It's going to be amazing," I said.

"It's a coincidence because I used to live in Akasaka, in your neighborhood and next door to Roppongi. I come here a lot with customers and I love this place."

"Cool. I'm just glad that you and I can actually have a normal conversation. It's been brutal in the office where no one really talks to each other," I said as a man approached us with three small, warm, and moist towels rolled up on a bamboo tray. He bowed profusely to Taka and kneeled so that the top of his head was at Taka's shoulder level.

"Japanese people are shy. Too many rules and too much hierarchy. Get them drunk and they'll talk."

"Good advice. I'll remember that."

"First rule of dining in Japan — always start with a beer, then we can order food," Taka explained after ordering three *nama bīru* (draft beers).

"This is a traditional Japanese bar that serves small plates of food. *Izakaya* basically means 'sake house' in Japanese. I suggest we get some fresh sashimi to start, fresh homemade tofu, which is a specialty here, grilled vegetables and fish, and some barbequed beef. Then maybe some *soba* if we're still hungry," Taka proposed.

"All sounds great," Renee replied.

"Love seafood. No objections from us," I added. Famished, we would take anything.

With authority Taka dictated in Japanese his selection of dishes to the man who disappeared quickly like a ninja. Within a few minutes, another familiar face appeared and joined us in the booth. It was Hirori, another classmate who'd been in business school with us and who'd joined the energy giant Exxon Mobile in Japan. That was a pleasant surprise as neither Renee nor I had expected to see her there.

The drinks came shortly and we all raised a glass with a "*kanpai*" (cheers) to celebrate a mini reunion in Japan. It was very special for Renee and me to be received by a couple of classmates I'd known for some time and they were super helpful in giving us advice on how best to settle in.

"Second rule when dining in Japan is always to say '*Itadakimasu!*' This kind of means 'I receive' and is roughly equivalent to 'Have a nice meal!'" said Taka, explaining an essential Japanese etiquette.

"One says it even if dining alone and sometimes with a slight bow," Hirori added as the first plates arrived.

The food was exquisite: fresh, flavorful, and just the right quantity. The ambience was perfect, with two old friends from another era, a memorable start to our gastronomic journey in Tokyo. We were delighted with the service and high quality of food at this *izakaya* and vowed to go back soon.

"Third rule when dining in Japan is that at the end of the meal, one says, '*Gochisōsama deshita*' (It was a feast) to the staff, and to the chef if he's nearby, showing appreciation for the food and service." Taka continued with his cultural lesson.

"*Gochisōsama deshita*," we said in the direction of the chef and server as we walked out, feeling very satisfied.

We took the elevator down to the ground level and found the man who'd served us doing push-ups as we exited the elevator.

"He's thanking us for our business," Hirori explained. "It's a different kind of customer service in Japan."

It was a great evening. Things were a little strange in the office but I'd loved the *izakaya* experience with great food and excellent customer service. There was hope after all.

⛩

Another week went by and I got slightly more adjusted to my new home but it was too early to tell whether this job was going to live up to expectations. Although I'd grown up in a Presbyterian family with a father who is a devout Christian, I was never truly religious. I did however, say a few prayers over the first couple of weeks in the new country, wishing that all would go well. Open-minded and intrigued by *Shinto*, the unofficial national religion of Japan, I suggested to Renee that we pay a visit to the Meiji Shrine on her last day in Tokyo.

The Japanese people go to shrines to worship a large number of different deities and there are probably hundreds of shrines around Tokyo and all over the rest of Japan. People go to different shrines to pray for various purposes, including those for travel safety, fertility, prosperity, passing an exam, etc. You can usually find them in a beautiful, peaceful park or a tucked-away sanctuary hidden from this urban concrete jungle. The architecture, construction materials, and landscaping are very simple, modest, and they evoke a sense of harmony with nature.

"I can use all the help I can get," I said to Renee.

"Yeah, I know you can. I'd like to see the Meiji Shrine; I've heard good things about it. But I'm more interested in the cosplay."

"The cos who?" I asked.

"You know, young people dressed up in costumes, pretending they're anime characters, a stuffed animal, or something else. These people supposedly hang out at the entrance to the shrine." Renee was surprised and disappointed that I didn't know about cosplay.

"OK, I'm down with that. What d'you know about the Meiji Shrine?" I asked.

"Well, this is one of the most famous shrines in all of Japan and a popular tourist destination in Tokyo. It was built around the 1920s or '30s after the death of Emperor Meiji, a super-important emperor in Japanese history," Renee recited while pulling up her smartphone.

"I know about Meiji too. He ruled Japan for the second half of the 19th century and was credited for modernizing Japan by getting rid of the samurais. Basically, Japan transformed into an industrialized nation when he was in power."

"Haha, you knew that because you saw Tom Cruise in *The Last Sumurai*."

"Sure did. Great movie."

Renee continued. "And do you know the difference between a shrine and a temple?"

"Well, temples are of Buddhist origin heavily influenced by China and then Korea and are much more ornate, grandiose, and colorful and often have a burial section on the property for the deceased monks. The shrines, on the other hand, are mostly very small and unassuming wooden structures that are quite humble but elegant." I already knew this from having been through a cultural crash course about six months before arriving in Japan.

Renee and I visited the beautiful grounds of the Meiji Shrine which was just three short stops away in Harajuku on the Chiyoda subway line. At the entrance we did see a group of youngsters decked out in anime costumes with blue and pink hair and lots of piercings. A short walk along the unpaved road, rows of empty wine barrels were stacked up on both sides of the pathway, apparently gifts from a former French king to the Japanese emperor. We then saw a massive, red Shinto torii gate, symbolic of the religion, standing about 15 meters tall and made of top-quality cypress from Taiwan. A few hundred meters later, a smaller but similar torii indicated the roughly halfway point to the shrine.

Near the entrance to the shrine was a water feature to wash your hands and cleanse your mouth as people are encouraged to follow the tradition before entering any shrine. We were lucky to witness a traditional Japanese wedding procession in the shrine that day with the wedding party dressed in kimonos typical of an older era, led by a priest wearing ten-centimeter platform sandals and holding an oversized, red parasol big enough for a family of four. The bride's hair was done like an actress in a *Kabuki* (Japanese dance-drama) show and she wore a white hat about twice as big as her head. The bride had a traditional Japanese wedding kimono, mostly white with an elegant floral outer layer bursting with bright colors of red and orange, while the groom's kimono was a black top and gray pant-skirts. Both bride and groom were wearing traditional white sandals. The couple and their family members strolled slowly around the shrine.

In the background two huge banyan trees about four stories tall had been deified and stood in the courtyard with hundreds of "wishes" written on small wooden plates hanging on their branches. Visitors and worshippers from all over Japan and some from abroad had placed their requests to the gods, hoping to pass an exam, get a new job, or something else.

"This is very special," Renee said.

"Agree. I should make some wishes and hang them on the tree."

"Better hope the Japanese gods understand English," she remarked.

"I'm sure they're well-trained in many languages by now; just look at all these foreigners here."

"So you're giving up your religion and turning Shinto?"

"I was never that religious, except for a brief time when I was a teenager. This is just about going with the flow. You know, when you're in Rome, or when you're in Tokyo..."

With that, I wrote on a couple of huge wooden plates, hoping for a fun-filled, unforgettable, and adventurous three years during my stay in Japan that would enrich our lives...or something to that effect.

We stood in wonder and took copious amounts of photos of the place with its hundreds, perhaps thousands, of wishes hanging from those majestic banyan trees. Momentarily forgetting where I'd come from and ignoring everything about work, I felt calm, peaceful, and optimistic in this sanctuary for worship and reflection.

Episode 5 (Go): Finding Ramen

After Renee left Tokyo to return to her law classes in NYC, I wandered around the streets of Akasaka in the evenings after work to explore the neighborhood. We tried our best to connect by Skype daily, my early evenings and her early mornings, me to report my daily adventures and Renee to tell me what was happening on the home front. The master plan was for Renee to finish her second year of law school in New York and then transfer to an American school that had a campus in Tokyo.

"What were the highlights for this week?" Renee asked on one of our calls.

"Well, no one is talking to me yet but I ate at a cool Belgian restaurant and beer hall called Delirium in the nearby Akasaka Sakas, you know that upscale shopping area and office complex right next to TBS where TV and film celebrities hang out? I drank some fancy, $15 bottle of beer brewed by monks to go with the delicious steamed mussels and sausages."

"That sounds good but why would you go Belgian when you're in Tokyo?" Renee asked.

"I knew you'd say that. I realized halfway through eating that I was being ridiculous for not eating sushi with sake or slurping on some *ramen* and chasing it with *shōchū* (fermented, clear liquor usually made from potatoes or other types of grain). I made up for it by patronizing a few different *ramen* shops the next few nights." I was ready for the interrogations and had my defense ready.

"Isn't all *ramen* the same?"

"No way! They're all slightly different as you can get different soups such as fatty, pork-based, fish-based or miso (soybean paste) broths. Different regions of Japan produce different types of noodles too. Funny thing is, I pretended that I was a local and walked into each place like I was a regular saying nothing but '*dōmo*' (hello) and pointed to a picture on the menu and said '*kore*' (this one) to the server. I focused on devouring my noodle, pickled vegetables, pieces of pork, and sometimes an egg, all in ten minutes or less and I spoke to no none. It's what you do in these noodle shops."

"I'm sorry you have to eat alone. Have you tried making some dinner at home?" Renee asked.

"Sure. It's already getting a little old eating out this whole week. One night I decided to have take-out sushi and sashimi and bought some miso paste to make the soup from ingredients bought in Yoshike, the mini-supermarket down the hill that's known for its selection of fresh fish. It's worked out well and much more economical."

"And what other exciting things did you do besides feeding yourself?" Renee continued her round of questioning.

"I don't know if they're exciting but I did open up two bank accounts, one at Citibank Japan for our personal banking needs and one at Sumitomo for work-related transactions. I learned that the company pays employees $50 a day when they travel overseas and that money gets deposited into the work account. So, I guess I should never eat alone while traveling because I can only expense a meal when eating with a colleague or customers. Also, I found out that my company will reimburse all our utility bills and they get deposited into Citibank."

"Sweet! That's very exciting."

"I also got a *hanko* (personal seal) as a surrogate for my signature.

I had to do this for opening up the bank accounts. It's compulsory in Japan and very old school," I went on.

"I know about the *hanko*. It's a tradition that came from China originally, centuries ago, where a stamp of your name with the seal is the same as your signature and it means you've approved whatever the document might be." Having lived in China, Renee required no explanation on this one.

"The only problem is, the *hanko* is literally more 'official' than your autograph. I had to make a couple of changes on our bank account and they wouldn't let me do the transaction because I didn't have my *hanko* with me, even though I had all kinds of documents in person to verify my identity," I said with amusement and frustration.

"You gotta be kidding me!" Renee exclaimed.

"No. And all you can do in a situation like that is say 'I understand' and respect the local rules."

For the ensuing weeks, I reminded myself that flexibility and adaptability are absolutely essential when living abroad. Having the right attitude, an open mind, and an adventurous spirit are advantageous and would allow you to not only survive but thrive in a foreign country. You may not be able to do much with the environment or circumstances, but how you decide to react to them will determine whether you'll have an incredibly good time or a miserable stay away from home.

Having been an immigrant twice in my life and having moved to a different city, state, or country over ten times in the fifteen years prior, I was no stranger to living amongst unfamiliar cultures and being in new environments. Yet with all the prior experiences living and traveling abroad and a great attitude, I wasn't immune to the occasional discomfort and sometimes displeasure of being in Japan because of my own biases and some hard-wired beliefs.

"Anything new at home?" I asked Renee.

"Same old. Studying non-stop. The cat misses you. I sold your car," Renee reported.

"Good. I don't miss the car one bit. I love taking trains to work and everywhere else. I also feel healthier already because I'm now eating mostly vegetables, fish, and overall smaller serving portions."

"Great. It's good for your blood sugar. Maybe you don't need those pills your doctor asked you to take after all?" Renee queried.

"I never filled the prescription and I feel fine. I also really enjoy the down-sized living spaces, minimal personal possessions, and a more active lifestyle overall."

"I'm happy you like your new lifestyle. How about the language thing? Did you finally start Japanese lessons?" Renee asked.

"*Hai. 'Dōmo Arigatō*, Mr. Roboto,'" I sang my response.

"What?"

"You know, that funky little tune by Styx about robots with some Japanese words thrown in, with a heavy synthesizer. I've had this song in my head for weeks and I couldn't get rid of it," I explained.

"I didn't ask you if you watched the Styx video on YouTube. I meant did these Japanese *sensei* (teachers) start going to your office twice a week to give you lessons as you told me?" Renee was a little thrown off by my reply and wasn't amused.

"Yeah, I know. They did. I mastered both katakana and hiragana alphabets in less than a month on my own. Last week Miyagi Sensei came to the office to start giving me formal lessons."

"And how's that going so far? More useful and real than *Rosetta Stone*?" Renee asked.

"Of course. Self-study never beats actual conversations. I've also been watching a lot of Japanese TV to try to figure out what's going on. Unfortunately, they dub almost everything here. The other day I watched an entire James Bond movie in Japanese and managed to understand just about everything."

"*Ohayō gozaimasu*, Bond-san. *Hajimemashite. Nomimono wa, ikaga desu ka*? (Good morning Bond. Nice to meet you. Would you like a drink?)"

"*Matīni, onegaishimasu* (please)."

"Well no one really needs to understand the dialogue in a movie where they're constantly blowing things up and where he saves the Bond girl with over-the-top stunts," Renee replied with a touch of sarcasm. "What are some of the practical things you've learned so far?"

"There are about ten different ways to say 'thank you,' of which '*dōmo arigatō*' is one safe and polite way. So, when in doubt, say '*dōmo arigatō*.' 'Mr. Roboto' is optional."

"Right. How about pronunciation? Seems like they use a lot of English words but always add a vowel at the end where there's none in English."

"That's right. The whole katakana writing system is devoted to words of foreign origin, including English. For example, '*tēburu*' is for table, '*toire*' is for toilet, and '*dezāto*' is for dessert, etc. My favorite has been '*Makudonarudo*' for Macdonald's," I continued my explanations.

"Sounds good. So, if you're craving a Big Mac, you can go to *Makudonarudo* and order a *Biggumakku* once you're there? OK, I have to say *sayōnara* now as it's time to leave to catch the train to NyūYōku." Renee got it fast.

Episode 6 (Roku): The Yakusa and the Sararīman

Akasaka, where I lived, had had a reputation for having a sleazy nightlife but had cleaned up its image in the years prior to my moving there. It's strategically located just a kilometer or so from the National Diet (Congress or Parliament), right next to the Imperial Palace compound, and is home to many embassies. Two very busy backstreets with names I can never remember are packed with bars, restaurants, and many other types of businesses to entertain everyone from your average *sararīman* (salary man) to the government officials and foreign dignitaries and their important guests on a variety of occasions. The establishments that stood out for me were the 'boutique hotels' Renee and I had stumbled upon, one of which had a woman dressed in a Playboy bunny outfit to attract guests. I'd also had some stares from men who would look at Renee (a tall, blue-eyed, blonde-haired, attractive, slim Caucasian) and then at me, and back to Renee. I knew what they were thinking: *How much did this guy pay for that young Russian prostitute and how can I get me some?*

Wanting to get some advice from the locals, I asked Ian for some intel and suggestions on the place I would call home for three years.

"So, tell me more about my neighborhood. What should I do there?" I asked Brewer-san.

"Well the question is what can you *not* do in Akasaka? It's a neighborhood built to entertain VIPs from politicians to celebrities and foreigners. You can get a massage, go to a karaoke, eat *ramen*, drink at an English pub or an upscale wine bar, and find a geisha all on the same night."

"OK, sounds good. I've seen ladies dressed in a white coat standing outside those shops, looking like legitimate therapists hawking their services. But tell me, what are all these Bentleys and Ferraris doing there?"

"It's a bit of an exclusive neighborhood with diplomats, big-time businesses, and a large number of Americans living there. A lot of wealth overall, that's why there's a Porsche and Ferrari dealership there. It's only in recent years that people started to live there as it was primarily a place to work and where the real estate had been untouchable for most Tokyoites. You're pretty damn lucky to be living there."

"I do feel lucky. And I figured it's a ritzy area because the other day, I walked out of my apartment building and saw a $300,000 Maybach parked across the street. Definitely not what I'm used to."

Ian went on. "It's a rich people's playground. During the old days, you would also see a lot of geishas in your neighborhood."

"Are they considered high-class prostitutes?"

"Ha. No, not at all. That's a common misconception. They're simply very well-trained entertainers skilled at different Japanese arts, such as playing classical Japanese music, dancing, and poetry. They don't sleep with customers, or they're not supposed to," Ian explained.

"Come to think of it, I think I've seen at least one lady all decked out in an elaborate kimono and walking in her colorful platform sandals entering one of these old wooden houses."

"Yes, you can still see them strolling in the alleyways of Akasaka. My guess is that there's still a demand for the geishas and their services, thus the few small, traditional Japanese wooden houses that still exist around Akasaka."

"Is it true that the *Yakusa* (Japanese mafia) still run many of these businesses in Akasaka?" I continue to pepper Ian with questions.

"The *Yakusa* are everywhere. They're not too hard to spot as they're usually in an entourage, have tattoos everywhere, occasionally a missing pinky, and much younger and attractive ladies accompany them."

"Isn't that like everywhere else? You know, the part about the entourage, the tattoos, and young ladies? Just like the Mafia in New York, the Triad in L.A., and the Russian gangs in Chicago?" I responded.

"Yes, except they don't typically carry firearms; it's rare. And therefore, there isn't much homicide. Overall, the crime rate's so low in Japan, the police are bored most of the time," Ian explained now with sarcasm.

"Alright, so I should steer clear of the guys with tattoos and missing fingers and maybe stick with *ramen* shops and massages?"

"They're harmless, for the most part. There's always Hooters if you miss your American sports bar. And if you want Korean barbeque, you're in the right place as there's a very large Korean-Japanese community there."

With that enlightening description from Ian, I had the place scoped out. Never a shortage of places to eat, to relax, and to entertain. It was a tamer version of Roppongi, as I would soon discover.

⛩

Through an online introduction by an American friend and former colleague, Brooke, I made a new friend, Joe, in Tokyo. Joe was a fellow American expat who coincidentally also started his assignment just a few days after I'd arrived in Japan. He worked for a rival drug firm a block away from me on the same street in the heart of the Pharmaville on Showa-dori.

"Hey, Joe, look forward to meeting you soon. Why don't we meet up at the Starbucks and decide where to go afterwards?" I emailed Joe one day.

"Done! See you around 7 p.m," Joe replied almost immediately.

"D'you have a photo on LinkedIn? Just making sure I can find you," I asked, just in case.

"I've seen your profile and the photo and I can pick you out. You'll know when you see me," Joe responded.

Starbucks was situated in glitzy Roppongi Hills where he lived. Roppongi Hills is the quintessential hangout for the rich and famous but also the hot spot for expats because English is widely spoken and understood in this ultra-modern and posh section of town filled with fancy shops, restaurants, bars, and various types of entertainment from the classy to the sleazy.

The trouble with Starbucks there, as it is in the U.S., is that there could be several on the same street block. Both of us were new and somewhat illiterate in Tokyo so I naturally went to the one that I thought was *the* one (out of three or four) in Roppongi and Joe went to all the other ones where he thought I would be. I had no idea what the man looked like so it was a bit of a guessing game. Half an hour past our meeting time, I got anxious and ordered a coffee from a barista.

"Latte, *onegaishimasu*." said the barista to a lady behind her.

"Latte," said the lady behind the barista to the crew in the back.

"Latte," Two or three more people said it once more, this time in unison.

I didn't know so much confirmation was needed just to make a coffee. I gave the cashier a ¥10,000 bill (roughly $100) and she said out loud, "*Ichi-man yen desu* (¥10,000, the biggest bill in Japanese currency)," and quickly turned around to show another lady, who I presumed was her supervisor. She then took out a ¥5,000 note, four ¥1,000 notes, and the rest of the change in coins. She patiently counted the change out loud, flicking each bill so I could see it clearly, before placing them onto a faux leather tray for me to retrieve.

Wow! What an elegant but laborious process. I liked it. In the U.S., they would hand you the change and say, "Next!"

In Japan, money is never handed directly to the customers. (That would be rude!) It's always presented on a tray, even when you take a taxi or at the convenience store. All this is done with a sustained, well-trained smile and a slight bow and a warm thank you at the end. I was impressed by the level of attention and service, all for a cup of coffee.

"Joe, it's Marcus. You're still coming?" I finally called Joe to make sure that he hadn't forgotten.

"Yeah, man. I've gone to three Starbucks stores and didn't see you but I'm sure you're in the next one I'm headed to." And before I could say another word, Joe came into the store I was at. I knew immediately it was him, as he'd predicted, as he headed immediately in my direction as soon as he spotted me.

"I need a cocktail after all that work trying to find you," Joe said with a smile.

"I know just the place. Why don't we go to Orange in Tokyo Midtown, which is just a couple of blocks away?" I proposed, having walked by the place but never been inside.

"I'm game. So where are you from?" Joe asked as we walked out of the coffee shop.

"New Jersey, most recently."

"Get out of here! I'm from New Jersey but I've lived in Chicago for many years. What a coincidence."

"Where in New Jersey?" I asked.

"Clifton. You know it?"

"Sure. Small world. It's near where I was living."

"So, what brought you out here?" Joe asked.

"Believe it or not, I've always wanted to do this. You know, experiencing another culture while on assignment, living the expat life. Took much longer than expected for it to happen, and in a different country than what I had in mind, but I'm thrilled to be in Tokyo. How about you?"

"Similar story. I've worked for this Japanese company for a while and spent two months in Osaka before. They liked me a lot and asked me to move here for a couple of years. I said yes," Joe said casually.

"I think it's a life-changing assignment and we're both pretty fortunate to be here," I responded in a serious tone.

"Yeah, I think years from now we'll look back and marvel at the experiences that we're about to have."

Being a single guy, Joe quickly changed the conversation topic and shared his view that Japanese women are some of the most exotic and attractive ladies in the world. I was married and so I deflected the comment with my admiration for the simple yet sophisticated style of traditional Japanese architecture. I nursed my glass of red wine while Joe had three beers as we talked, clearly thirsty. I had a feeling we were quite different but that we were going to get along just fine. As we parted, we made plans to hit the town together that weekend.

Episode 7 (Nana): Work-Life Balance

A month into my assignment and I validated my belief that the Japanese people are the politest I know on the planet. Bowing is common in Japan, as most people know, but seeing it in action and doing it was a new experience. It was so excessive and uncomfortable at times. I do think however, that Americans could take a cue from the Japanese and act more politely more often. Whether you're at a fancy restaurant or a 7-Eleven, the Japanese always appear so happy to see you and aim to provide exceptional customer service.

At an upscale *shabu-shabu* (hot pot) place I went to one night with Renee, the store manager saw us off after we finished our meal and bowed 45 degrees and stayed in that position until we could no longer see him. I knew because I turned around a couple of times to check, the first time at ten meters away and then just before we went down the escalator. Yep, the man was taking no chances. To learn more about this etiquette, I asked Ian for some guidance to make sure I didn't offend anyone unintentionally.

"Well, amongst colleagues, bowing is expected when you simply want to ask him or her a question. You should bow again when the discussion finishes," Ian explained.

"How about this expression: 'Thank you for your cooperation?' I was slightly confused in the beginning after someone said this to me, thinking that they didn't expect me to cooperate. The only time you hear that in the U.S. is if you're being interviewed as a witness by a policeman for something related to a crime but I hear it regularly here."

"Ha. Don't worry. Everyone says that to each other. It's polite. It's a direct translation from Japanese. We live in a socialist society and we cooperate. It's just their custom to thank people." He added, "Here are a couple more rules about bowing. Always bow deeper to someone more senior than you. If someone did a favor for you, you would be bowing a very long and deep bow. And God forbid, if you make a huge mistake and need to apologize to save your job, you might need to touch the ground with your forehead, palms, knees, and feet." Ian was getting to the good stuff.

I would find myself nodding my head constantly for the first few weeks (it's an abbreviated and much more common form of bowing) and I would start to build a strong set of neck muscles I didn't know existed.

Ian continued with his cultural lessons. "Another example of being polite, but a controversial one that's more of a double-edged sword, is that the Japanese would almost never say 'no' to you. The word exists in the Japanese language but they avoid it like the plague rather than be impolite, disappoint, insult, and just want to leave room for a positive interpretation."

"For example?" I asked.

"Well, when you're in a shoe store with a store clerk and you ask for your shoe size, which they probably don't have, they're *not* going to tell you they don't have it."

"What d'you mean? What would they say instead?"

"*Aaaah, ima, chotto...* That literally means 'right now, a little...' But what it actually means is a big fat, 'No.' The word *chotto* (little) is used all the time for polite refusal; makes no sense and it took a while for me to get it too." He went on. "In the office, if you ask a colleague if he would like to go for a beer after work, a likely response could be '*Muzukashī desu ne.*' And that means, 'Ah, it's difficult.' But it also means 'No, at least not with you.' And finally, if you're trying to return something you bought from a department store and they make this sucking 'Sssssssss' sound, that unequivocally means 'HELL NO!'"

That five-minute tutorial in Japanese etiquette was illuminating and frustrating. No wonder I hadn't heard anyone saying "*iie*" (no) to me for a month. I suspected that I wouldn't hear it anytime soon.

⛩

In my previous employer's home office, the second and third Wednesday of every month was "Work-Life Balance Day." Having embraced some of the Western customs and trying to address work-life "imbalance" issues typical of Japan, the company I was now working for had adopted this euphemism of a rule. The first time I heard the announcement "*Kyō wa, Wāku-Raifu Baransu De desu*" (Today is Work-Life Balance Day), I wasn't quite sure what was happening, where I was, or how to react to it. It came through the loudspeakers on the ceiling, with a xylophone-sounding, synthesizer-generated intro music. I thought that we were being asked to evacuate the building because of a fire alarm. I was half right about the evacuation part.

I'd been fighting the late afternoon stupor, partially caused by the deafening silence in the office where people preferred staring at the computer screen over speaking to human beings. I would drink copious amounts of that repulsive free green tea from the lounge and type loudly to stay awake. The sound that suddenly emerged from the loudspeakers was strangely familiar and nostalgic and prompted me to listen for something about special items on sale at a Kmart store or flight departure information. Instead I heard the words "*Wāku-Raifu Baransu*" then gibberish followed from the HR department at 5:30 p.m. sharp, asking everyone to ditch their work (real or pretend) promptly and to head to the nearest exit.

"You need to leave." Ian turned to me with a smirk and delivered the command.

"Pardon me?"

"Today's Work-Life Balance Day and we leave at 5:30." Ian was packing his things and putting on his jacket.

"Right. But no one's moving." I scanned the floor and most people seemed to have missed the announcement.

"Wait five minutes if you want then get out of here. You shouldn't stay. You would send a wrong message and that wouldn't be good. Besides, the HR swat team will be here shortly to harass people to go and you don't want to get on their bad side."

"If they want people to have good balance, why don't they let people work from home one day a week or something, like we do in the States?" I asked.

"There's no such thing here. It's a fantasy and people wouldn't know what to do with themselves at home. This is Japan. Old school."

A group of six HR folks did in fact show up almost immediately, all wearing a white band on their sleeves with large bold kanji characters that said "*Jinji*" (Human Resources). They started going around the floors to pester employees if they stayed too long at their desks.

"In Japan, HR folks have a lot of power in a corporation, more so than those folks in Marketing or Sales who generate the revenue for companies. No one wants ever to cross HR because they can decide whether you'll be enjoying a glamorous expat assignment in America (or another destination of your choice) or be driving a delivery truck in frigid Sapporo on your next job." With that elegant explanation, Ian promptly headed for the elevator.

Sure enough, about a minute later, a *buchō* (department VP) who sat at a desk facing his rows of subordinates got up and a few of people started to pack up almost immediately to follow their leader. Ian was a fine role model for always leaving right on time or soon after the bell rang, which sent a clear signal to my department that it was OK to leave soon.

Our intrepid leader Yamamoto-san however, was another story. He was always there when I got in between 8:00 to 8:30 a.m. and was still there when I left around 6 p.m. The rumor was that he only slept on Sundays and worked around the clock, which was probably why he always looked half asleep (or half awake). Whatever the case may be, he clearly had mastered the art of Zen meditation at work and could transition in and out of it. I didn't want to upset the mighty HR department so I promptly left with Ian soon after.

What a country!

Episode 8 (Hachi): The Beer Conspiracy

Almost two months in, life was starting to take on a degree of normalcy and routines started to emerge. I'd found the optimal way to commute to work after being confused initially by the seven subway entrances to four different train lines all within a ten-minute walk. For food, I would go to Yoshike down the hill for fresh fish and other weekly dietary essentials for the fridge. Hanamasa, just around the corner from Yoshike, was the place for rice, pasta, and meats at wholesale prices. I also discovered the 24-hour foreigner-friendly supermarket called Precce in the Midtown Tower where you could find just about everything from home but at a premium price.

One evening as I was preparing dinner in the kitchen, I felt the ground move. I noticed the ripples in the glass of water I had right next to me. A plate glided a few centimeters along the granite countertop and touched the glass with a bang as the shaking got stronger. I was in the middle of chopping some onions and barely missed slicing a piece of flesh on my left index finger. I dropped the sharp Henckels knife, stood still, and took in a long, deep breath. It was an earthquake.

"Don't panic," I told myself. "This'll pass and my building was built with state-of-the-art, earthquake-proof technology so I don't need to worry." Nevertheless, a level of concern started to develop after what felt like an eternity and one of the framed photos on the wall fell to the ground, smashing the glass. The 15-story building swung side to side for nearly a minute and I remained still like a flagpole the entire time. Finally, it stopped.

I sat on the couch for a while after that dinner interruption and tried to devise a plan in the event it happened again. It hadn't been a pleasant experience.

"So, what other adventures did you have this week besides the tremor?" Renee asked during our regular Skyping session.

"I went to the Kinokuniya bookstore in Shinjuku and got a bilingual Japanese cooking book. I've been making simple stuff like *wakame* (a type of seaweed) salad and miso soup and grilling fish using the kick-ass built-in grill that sits just beneath the gas stove in the kitchen."

"Great! Did you get that microwave? That would make heating up things easier," Renee asked

"Funny you should ask. Our Yankees-crazed landlord finally had someone drop off a microwave that doubles as a roaster the other day. It worked most of the time but was way over-engineered with some 30 functional buttons, half of which I couldn't understand and the manual in Japanese is a few centimeters thick."

"What kind of fish are you grilling?"

"I do a lot of *saba* (mackerel) fillets, which strangely came from a farm in Norway. It's cheap and tasty and rich in Omega-3. I ate so much *saba* I'm pretty sure that my mercury level has at least tripled since I arrived in Japan," I said, halfway joking.

"What else? Did you try some of those mysterious condiments?" Renee asked.

"Yep. I tried cooking with *mirin*, a typical Japanese staple that's a mixture of vinegar, sake, and other sweet ingredients. I also discovered a popular local spice mixture called *sichimi* (seven flavors) and quickly took a liking to it. I've been putting that magic powder on most of the meats I made and into the soup noodles."

"Sounds tasty. And the beers? Seems like a compulsory drink in Japanese social settings. Any new favorite brews?"

"Well, probably Yebisu Premium. It's very popular in Japan, probably because of all the commercials by celebs. But I think it's very expensive because each can costs over $2.00 in a supermarket. I think it's a bit of a conspiracy and a protectionist move by the Japanese government."

"What d'you mean?"

"I mean I haven't seen any American beers in the Japanese market; no Budweiser or Bud Light, Miller Lite, or the equally awful Coors Light that dominate the U.S. I'm not a big beer drinker and no expert but for me these Japanese lagers are tastier probably because they were brewed longer, with lots more hops, and with a technique that's heavily influenced by the Germans. I'm pretty sure I've drunk more beer in three months than I did all last year."

"So, you're not going out much at night anymore?"

"No, it's expensive and I need to chill for a while. After dinner on a work night, I usually crash on that new leather couch to flip through lots of blasé channels in Japanese that I can't really understand. I've mastered the correct pronunciation of the names of all major Japanese cities from watching the weather channel and I've memorized the temperature ranges from Okinawa in the south to Sapporo in the north and for all the cities in between."

While I still enjoyed venturing out at night, mostly on my own, I was past the phase where I needed to do it very often. I enjoyed relaxing with *Animal Planet* although it was dubbed and the dogs barked in Japanese. I tried to make sense of a very popular, chaotic, and unpredictable entertainment show and was too distracted by the insane anime hair-dos and crazy pastel, plaid jackets worn by the androgynous host. Sitting in my fancy mansion in the middle of a bustling commercial neighborhood and feeling a bit sequestered, I began to understand why corporations compensate their expat employees very well with generous subsidies when they're sent to work abroad for a while. The need to deal with all the inconveniences of being in an exotic land where not speaking the language or knowing the local culture could be quite difficult. The bigger challenge, in my opinion, is leaving behind friends and family back home and having to give up (at least temporarily) an essential support network which is important for anybody home or abroad.

"What's new at the office?" Renee switched the subject.

"Ha. That's a depressing topic. I stopped trying to have conversations with my colleagues during lunch. After the quick calorie intake, I like going to the Maruzen bookstore, getting some air, and vitamin D from the sun. I sometimes walk by the café where Ian said he would be and I see him puffing away and focusing intently on his crossword puzzles with a pen in hand at a seat by the window. I occasionally stand right in front of him outside the glass and he won't even notice me."

"That sounds funny, and lonely."

"Well, no. To each their own. I manage to stay busy and entertained. At the upscale Maruzen, I can see the latest bestsellers in English and I like to browse through the hundreds of *manga* on the shelves. I actually bought some simple Japanese *manga* to help me practice my Japanese."

"What did you get?"

"A couple of books called *Doraemon*, a hugely popular kids' comic book in Japan and many parts of Asia that have been around since the late '60s. This is familiar and nostalgic for me as I used to watch its cartoon as a young child living in Asia some 30 years ago."

"Is this the robotic cat with a built-in pouch full of gadgets?" Renee asked.

"You know it?"

"Yeah, because I saw it in Beijing when I lived there. It has a different name in Mandarin. The main character travels back from the future to solve every imaginable problem that his master has. His master is this awkward pre-teen boy who isn't very good in school and admires the girl next door and would do everything to win her over. Right?" Renee has photographic memory.

"I'm impressed."

Renee continued. "Did you try the food halls in the department store?"

"Of course! I like Takashimaya department store across the street from Maruzen. I usually do a quick stroll through since the items I fancy would cost me a month's salary. But I like going down to the basement to check out the massive selection of foods and desserts in the stalls. My favorites are grilled red-bean bun or fresh *mochi*." (*Mochi* is a traditional Japanese rice-cake dessert of glutinous rice with a sweet filling, usually red bean or white bean paste, and has a soft and sticky texture.)

"Yummy. And what did you do for Valentine's Day? I mean I got your card. But what do they do to celebrate there?" Two questions in that one probe.

"Oh yeah. I spent Valentine's Day alone in an Irish bar called the Dubliner and had two Guinnesses to wash down some fatty sausages and chips. The interesting part is the tradition for the Japanese women to give chocolate to their boyfriends, husbands, or special friends and even male co-workers on February 14th. Boys as young as five or six will get them in kindergarten." I found this cultural snippet interesting.

"So, the men do nothing?" Renee sounded a bit annoyed.

"Not quite. The Japanese business people were clever and invented a twist on this tradition by adding a follow-up 'White Day' a month later where men return the favor by giving their significant others a gift or perhaps a nice dinner or something else. Great custom, I thought, where both parties get and give something." Speaking like the businessman that I am.

"I see. That's much better. What did your female co-workers bring?"

"In the office, Murayama-san brought homemade chocolate to the department to share with everyone on the team. She had been bringing *giri choco* (obligatory chocolate) since she joined the team seven or eight years prior. The *giri choco* is very common in the workplace although I heard that in many places, this nice tradition has been downgraded and admins now go to a 7-Eleven to pick up a box of pre-packaged chocolate or candy and call it a day."

The handing out of the sweets in the office occurs about 3 p.m., almost on the dot, whether it's Valentine's Day *choco* or any other *omiyage* (souvenirs) that you'd bring back from a business trip. This bringing and sharing of *omiyage* with office staff is also a fine custom and everyone is conditioned like Pavlov's dog to expect a treat mid-afternoon at least once a week.

⛩

For the first time since arriving in Japan, I went to a Thunderbird alumni function organized every month called First Tuesday at Suji's in Roppongi, a popular venue with expats near the Russian Embassy and the American Club. It was an upscale café owned by a Korean-American lady, Suji-san, who spent many years in New York City and had decorated the place with many black and white posters of NYC landmarks such as the Chrysler Building and the Brooklyn Bridge. A familiar dish when you went through bouts of home-sickness, an American style *hanbāgā* could be had for a hefty $20 or a homemade meatloaf or nachos for $15.

There I met Yoshi, the chapter president who was a professional golfer and fellow rugby player. I started to come to life after meeting more than a dozen other people, Thunderbirds and their friends, and reminisced about the good old times on campus. After some initial round-robin meet and greet, the crowd gradually and unfortunately separated into two cohorts, the Japanese t-birds plus their spouses and the other much smaller group of just *gaijin* t-birds. I hit it off with an American accountant and a man whose profession was vague and we had a great night drinking way too many *nama bīru* and swapping silly expat stories about being one of few *gaijin* in the office.

Episode 9 (Kyū): Subway Fashion

"So, are you settling in alright?" Ian asked me one day, unexpectedly.

"All good. Getting to know the neighborhood, learning some Japanese, and the commute is easy — five stops, straight shot," I replied.

"That's the understatement of the year. You probably win the award for having the shortest commute in the company. It's a dream. Most of these people here, including myself, are in the train for at least an hour each way."

"Can't complain. The trains are super crowded and there are some questionable odors but they're clean and run like clockwork."

"This is Japan. They're on time all the time, even with hundreds of trains running through the heart of Tokyo every day. The only exception is when some poor bastard decides to take his own life by stepping in front of a moving train, which unfortunately happens more often than expected."

Between the subway trains, commuter lines, and the famed *Shinkansen* (bullet train), there were more than 70 rail lines in metropolitan Tokyo at the time, transporting more than ten million passengers daily; three million going through the Shinjuku Station alone every day. After some trial and error, I found the quickest way to the station for my daily commute to Nihonbashi. During the weekday mornings, I would go down the hill to the right of my mansion building onto the alleyway with no name, cut through the Akasaka Twin Towers, and descend to the lower level to get to entrance/exit 12 at Tameike Sannō station on the Ginza line, the oldest subway line in Japan. On the way to the platform, I would pass about half a dozen coffee shops including a Starbucks, a 7-Eleven, three Japanese banks, a French bakery, and at least three other convenience stores. I would walk through this 150m-long walkway, facing the march of hundreds of *sararīman* in the opposite direction since most people were coming to my neighborhood to work.

"The only surprise for me so far," I told Ian, "is that I don't see those platform attendants pushing commuters into really crowded trains during rush hour. I saw the videos on YouTube and fully expected to be pushed."

"Ah, that's been banned recently because of complaints by female riders. Groping had been a problem for ladies riding in severely congested trains where some men, frequently government employees, made more bodily contact with female commuters than necessary," Ian explained.

"I see. That's a lawsuit waiting to happen in the States. Some might even get shot at, given so many people carry a concealed weapon."

"Not here, cowboy, not in this culture. Previously people ignored it and put up with being pushed around while not looking up but I think people are fed up, especially the women. That's why you see some female-only carts and platform attendants can no longer push people into the trains." Ian was very up-to-date with policy.

One phenomenon was the large number of people who wore a white surgical mask, at least one in four. They did that to cover their noses and mouths for fear of catching germs, or perhaps more accurately, to not spread their own to others. The other odd thing for me was everyone seemed to be scared to look at each other, as if it was a crime. For weeks I tried to make eye contact and smile to people everywhere I went in the metro walkways — in the train, on the streets, and in the stores — but hardly anyone ever returned the favor. I started to think that I was being impolite, aggressive, and perhaps deranged.

"Illegal eye contact, I hereby sentence you to 30 days in jail and a ¥100,000 fine." I imagined standing in a courtroom and a judge handing me the verdict.

I was determined however, to break down the stoic façade of the Japanese and overwhelm them with warm smiles and kindness but nothing worked. Eventually I resorted to meditating much of the time when I was commuting on the subway. I'd finished reading a book on meditation and breathing by the famous Vietnamese Zen Buddhist monk Thich Nhat Hanh.

Breathe in with the left foot to calm my body and breathe out with the right and I smile. I synchronized this technique with the announcements from the train.

Breathe in: *Kono densha wa Asakusa yuki desu.* (This train is going to Asakusa.)

Breathe out: *Takashimaya desu. Doa wa migi ni hirakimas. Tsugi wa, Mitsukoshimae.* (This is Takashimaya. The door will open on the right. Next stop, Mitsukoshimae.)

I'd memorized these pre-recorded phrases that blurted out from the speakers in the train and I could predict with precision when the announcements would be made and when doors would open at each station. I also tried to line up at the same spot on the platform at Tameike Sannō to get on cart six every day to have an easy exit at my destination at Nihonbashi. I started to recognize faces and I knew they recognized me as well: The middle-aged woman with orange hair who always wore a dead animal around her neck and sat next to a right-hand door in cart six. The fashionable young fellow always in a checked pattern gray suit with a pair of super-sized bug-eye glasses and anime hair straight out of Pokémon. And the older gentleman with the same argyle scarf and a limp who clutched onto a copy of *Asahi Shimbun* but with his eyes shut most of the time. Yet I knew we would never exchange words, not in that country sadly.

I read the advertisements in each cart and at each station and tried to guess what these campaigns were trying to convey since I didn't fully understand the language yet.

For Toranomon Station, it was the Yebisu beer ad with a smartly dressed middle-aged man, an actor apparently, with a silly grin and a far more attractive younger woman with a half-smile looking coy. I supposed the message was the same everywhere — if you drank beer, beautiful women in bikinis (or kimonos) would appear so there was no need to understand the copy of the ad.

At Ginza, the uber-posh shopping mecca of all of Japan, it was purses, purses, and more purses of haute couture with many brand names that I couldn't recognize or pronounce; quite evident that I wasn't the target demographic.

At Shinbashi, you would be lucky if you could breathe because legions of *salarīman* and *kyariaūman* (career women) rushed the gates and everyone braced for a tight squeeze and prepared to be groped. I'd always made a mental note to lean back there and to hold my breath for just a few seconds because I never knew if I was going to smell someone's eau de toilette or their breakfast, both of which could be overpowering. I learned this the hard way but fast.

⛩

To make time go by faster and for sheer entertainment, I started to play a game of statistics on my way to work, focusing on various categories but mostly on people's attire:

— Women wearing tall boots up to or past their knees: 35%. Those under age 30: 50%
— Women carrying a brand-name purse (Louis Vuitton, Gucci, or Burberry): 75%
— Women with their hair dyed: 50%. Those in red: 80% (It was a red year)
— Women with patterned stockings: 60%
— Men with anime hair: 35% (I had gone anime shortly after)

— Men with slim-fit suits (especially pants): 90% (They can pull this off because they weigh so little, they look as if they have a Body Mass Index of about 15)
— High school girls whose uniform skirts were too short, maybe 15-20 centimeters above their knees: 75%
— Men or women wearing a surgical mask: 30%

This last one wasn't a fashion statement but they made the masks interesting with colors and other designs featuring Hello Kitty and a host of other anime characters. Make no mistake, Tokyo is the fashion capital of Asia. For a culture so rich with its own history and heritage, the people are receptive to exotic things and foreign influences. Quite often they're quick to embrace the latest fashion trends and in some cases, set their own. Tokyoites live in tiny apartments and often stay with their parents to save money until they get married. Employers often subsidize their housing and they don't eat much. Most don't have a car so they splurge on expensive accessories and clothing.

Most of my former colleagues sported something nice on their wrists that was easily two to three times their monthly salary: Rolexes, Tags, and Omegas were the most popular brands. The Japanese are very much status conscious, loyal to branded products, and obsessed with high-quality items and services. They're a marketer's dream and they keep many European fashion houses in business. Creative marketers target college seniors about to graduate and offer flexible financing terms for their expensive timepieces. For the youngsters out of university, it wasn't uncommon to get a job and a Rolex at the same time. I remember feeling inadequate at first with my sleek but inexpensive Skagen and a classy but cheap Kenneth Cole; each had a retail value of about $100 and I'd got both from redeeming American Express credit card reward points.

I definitely didn't have my priorities in the same order.

Episode 10 (Jū): Team-Building Exercise

"I think the most exciting that's happened this week was the offsite meeting with my department," I told Renee in a Skype call. "We were supposed to strategize for the rest of the year and it was a real humdinger."

"What? Someone got drunk, said something inappropriate?"

"Well the first part was totally expected and the second was an eye-opener. But it was more than that. The whole thing was just very bizarre and uncomfortable, yet hilarious." I tried to summarize in a couple of sentences. "You met the head of our group, Yamamoto-san, who had decided that to be a truly global department, we must start acting like one, which is why he asked for all presentations from now on to be in English."

"That's great. But don't they all speak good English already? I mean you told me most of them studied or worked, or both, in the U.S. or Europe, right?" Renee asked.

"That's true but it was unusual and awkward for them to present to each other in English. I felt slightly guilty that they had to do this because of *gaijin* number two — me. Ian, who's been here for over ten years, is very proficient with Japanese and they'd gotten by with Japanese-only presentations and discussions until now," I explained.

"Well, it's not your fault. I meant Yamamoto is right that they need to man up if they want to be truly global marketers." Renee was being sensible.

"I don't disagree. I just felt bad because they really struggled and had stage fright, right at their seats. It wasn't a comfortable ride but luckily there were no fatalities."

"Haha. I'm sure they were speaking fluently after a few glasses of sake."

"Not only did they speak, they came to life during dinner at this overpriced, Japanized Chinese restaurant that was opened up by one of the original Iron Chefs. The food was great but the conversations that followed were hysterical."

"Sounds like dinner was the highlight of an otherwise bland and painful offsite meeting."

"I can write an article on cultural norms and faux pas, based on the offsite dinner. It's probably the climax of my assignment so far."

"People get drunk all the time and do stupid stuff. What's so different about this one?"

"You have no idea. For starters, we probably drank ten bottles of wine within our group of fifteen. The staff knew that Ian appreciates fine French wine from the Burgundy region and they made sure that the fermented grape juice flowed freely at dinner. That, by the way, was after we all had a compulsory round of beer. Some had two."

"OK, fast-forward to the good part."

"Wait, hold your horses. So, Ian did the obligatory cheer — 'Otsukaresama deshita' (Thank you for all your hard work) — and everyone had a gulp of beer. Then each person poured beer into another person's glass because it's very rude to fill your own glass at a dinner like this."

"Cool, but pretty tame so far."

"It got interesting because halfway through our eight-course meal, I noticed that our VP Yamamoto sitting to my left had his head cocked to the right, face bright red, and eyes closed."

"OK, that's amusing. And what did you do?"

"Well I looked around the table looking for signs of appropriate action but everyone just carried on as if nothing had happened. A few minutes later he was wide awake and he took a sip of his wine. What a leader!"

"And then?"

"So, we stuffed our faces, actually some were shit-faced after the dinner, with all that Burgundy in our bloodstream. You know what the Japanese are like — not drinking often then drinking too quickly when they do, just to get a buzz. I was ready to walk home and pass out until Yamamoto proposed that we all go next door to the French brasserie, Aux Bacchanales, for more team-building."

"And do what?"

"More drinks of course. Knowing he probably didn't convince anyone that he was up to the task, he asked Ian if he was interested. Ian immediately accepted the challenge, and with gusto. This is when all hell broke loose because everyone was completely wasted and too tired to think straight."

"Smells like trouble. Anyone get fired?" Renee was now totally engaged.

"Well if we were in the U.S., a lot of people would have, given the comments that were made to female employees. But this is Japan, and no one does."

I spent the next few minutes regaling Renee with the mayhem that had followed later that evening.

While in business school, I'd learned about the Abilene Paradox, which is when a group of people collectively decide or agree on a course of action that's counter to the preferences of many (or all) of the individuals in the group. This is common especially if the leader or someone with authority proposes it. I assumed that no one, with the exception of Ian, really wanted to do this, and that the VP simply felt obligated to take his troops through yet another round of bonding exercise. All but two of our group stuck around and the festivities moved next door. The two non-conformists still had their jobs the following Monday although I quickly learned that one guy was being transferred to Shanghai a few weeks later for three years and that the female colleague was looking for external opportunities. Coincidence these two didn't bother to join in? I think not.

With three more bottles of premier cru from Bourgogne, the after-party started in the smoky French brasserie and bar (and a damn good bakery during the day as well) where most of us were half asleep or hoping to be. A few American expats stared at the TV bolted high on a wall where the Super Bowl in the U.S. was being shown. Some of my Japanese colleagues did time in the U.S. subsidiary and understood American football so we watched the Steelers playing against the Cardinals with some interest. I went to grad school in Arizona so I was partial to the Cardinals although I wasn't aware they'd made it that far. Super Bowl? Must have been a bad joke, I thought initially, given the Cardinals had consistently been one of the worst teams in the league. We sipped the sour purple liquid and occasionally paid attention to an entertaining match and I tried my best to learn something personal about my team.

In Japan, people get to know each other outside the office when they're more relaxed and where true opinions are shared and many decisions are made. This was my second outing with the group and I expected more personal exchanges like what kinds of music they enjoyed, what hobbies they had, or where they hung out on weekends. By this time their inhibitions were just about gone and they became very chatty all of a sudden. After a few warm-up questions, Ono-san threw a few zingers at me.

"Chen-san, have you been to the maid café in Akihabara? You know those cafés where women are dressed in a French maid uniform and serve clients food and drinks? Some will also cut hair and give massages."

I was caught off guard. "Hmmm, I've been to Akihabara to buy a TV and I looked for a camera. I'd only heard of maid cafés. Anyway, I think I may be too old for that."

"How about the Kabuki-cho in Shinjuku (biggest red-light district in Japan)? You know you can eat sashimi from a naked woman's belly," Ono-san said with a big grin.

I looked over to my female colleague sitting next to me before I responded. "Well I've been to Shinjuku to eat and to shop but I've never heard of Kabuki-cho. And anyway, I'm not interested in that type of entertainment." I tried to be proper in my intoxicated state.

There were a couple more thought-provoking questions during the rapid-fire round of interrogation, all entirely inappropriate given the work-related setting. But one particular comment (or maybe it was a question, I wasn't sure) was memorable, when Ono-san said to the lady to my left, "I don't think you wear panties because I think you're a very natural woman."

For real?! You said that?!

I gasped, not entirely sure what I'd heard, and waited for someone to pounce. I was quite shocked because it was wrong in so many ways. In the U.S. I'd've expected that person to get fired the next day. My female colleague had no response but managed to produce a giggle, perhaps out of embarrassment bordering on bewilderment while trying her best to suppress her anger. Ian stepped in finally.

"You have to stop now, Ono-san. Have another drink," Ian, who was Ono's boss, said seriously, although the second part was counterintuitive.

Seconds later we all heard a loud bang as if someone had dropped a weighty object on the floor. Everyone turned their heads to search for casualties. We all quickly realized that it was Yamamoto who'd slammed his forehead onto the marble round table in front of where he sat. For the second time, everyone ignored what happened and carried on.

"*Sumimasen* (Sorry)," Yamamoto said and took another gulp of the Burgundy.

Fun was had by all, and the bond was strong but I didn't get to know my colleagues any better other than confirming that everyone has split personalities — one with alcohol, the other without. The next morning was business as usual, no small talk and as if none of this happened the night before. It was becoming obvious that this behavior was very typical of Japan.

I'm never gonna make it in this place.

⛩

A few days after the eventful evening offsite, I decided I needed to escape the city. I couldn't hang out with anyone from work and Joe had a prior engagement with a new lady friend so I was on my own.

"Ian, what cool place d'you suggest I go this weekend if I want to see some culture and history, somewhere away from the city but not too far?"

"I got the perfect place for you — Kamakura. Very charming historical town with about 20,000 inhabitants and only about an hour south of Tokyo by train," Ian advised.

"Yeah, I read about it in my guidebook. Didn't it used to be the capital of Japan, although short-lived?"

"Well depending on whether you think a century and a half is short. Back in the 12th century or so, the Minamoto clan gained control of much of Japan and built their capital city there. It was a smart move because the village is surrounded by mountains on three sides and the ocean on one side. Hard to attack." Not only is Ian a wine connoisseur but he's also full of Japanese historical trivia.

"I remember now. They started what became 700 years of military rule in Japan, dominated by the Shōguns. Yeah, I'd love to see it." A bit of a history buff myself, this was a no-brainer.

"If you're not tired of seeing temples and shrines, you'll see some beautiful works of art there, including some of the oldest Zen temples in Japan. If you do go, make sure to check out a famous *soba* shop that's a personal favorite of mine."

"I remember reading about a temple in the middle of a grove of giant bamboo trees where you can sit and contemplate the universe while sipping *macha* (whisked green tea). Have you been there?" I asked.

"I have. It's called Hokokuji, one of my favorite spots there. You should also check out the *Daibutsu* (Great Buddha). It's a bronze statute 13 meters tall and built more than seven centuries ago." Ian seemed to have played tour guide on many occasions.

Kamakura was my first encounter with the "Old Japan" and how

I'd pictured Japan as a kid growing up. I visited several of these well-known temples and shrines and I started to imagine life in a very different epoch. First stop was Hare-dera, with its pristine and traditional Japanese gardens with plum blossoms and ponds with many fat koi fish in them. It's known for having thousands of stone figurines call *jizo*, one of the most popular Buddhist divinities, offered in memory of deceased children and babies. At the top of the place is a perfect spot to have lunch overlooking Sagami Bay. I then proceeded to Tsurugaoka Hachimangū, a must-see in Kamakura and one of the biggest shrines with its imposing red torii gate. It's one of the most renowned shrines in Japan, built in 1063 and dedicated to the emperor Ojin who was then deified as Hachiman, the God of War.

I saw the imposing bronze *Daibutsu* and sipped *macha* in the Hokokuji and I thoroughly enjoyed it. My favorite place however, was the not so touristy temple of Jomyoji where monks came out to chant and pray for whatever I wished while I appreciated my *macha*. This was a perfect ending to a memorable trip. It was nearly closing time around four in the afternoon and few people remained on the premises. I sipped my *macha* on the *tatami* in the tea house looking out to a perfectly manicured Zen garden with raked sand simulating a pond.

I was shown a special way to turn the tea bowl and to sit in a posture called *seiza* where the knees touch the matt and the butt rests on the heels of the feet. I listened to water dripping slowly from a bamboo pipe into a wooden bucket, the only detectable sound around me, and I pondered the purpose of life. Time seemed to have slowed down and it was so quiet and peaceful that I questioned my very existence.

I had truly arrived in Japan.

Episode 11 (Jūichi): Open the Kimono

At work I'd stopped using typical business vocabulary and American expressions such as "going down a rabbit hole," "opening a can of worms," or "hitting one out of the park." This type of speech tended to turn my Japanese colleagues into deer and me the headlights of a car. Old habits die hard and I had to remind myself that English really is a funny language with so many common phrases that make no sense to non-native speakers. Even after having lived in five other countries and taken many cross-cultural communications courses, I relapsed occasionally and would say things like "stop beating around the bushes." The most horrifying thing to my Japanese co-workers was when I said, "Let's open the kimono." My female colleagues were especially horrified but I did get their attention.

I also started to go out to lunch a lot more, especially with fellow American expat Joe. Other lunch buddies included a couple of female colleagues from the fifth floor who had a perfect command of the English language. Kuroda-san, who worked in marketing with emerging markets, did her studies in the U.K. and spoke like a Londoner. And Takahashi-san, a tall and lanky lady in the International Business Department, was an amateur photographer who studied film in New York City. My favorite place was an excellent grilled *saba* place at a vintage Japanese wooden house that dated back to WWII era.

"So, Joe, what's new?" I asked him as we sat down on the *tatami* during one of these lunches at the *saba* house.

"You know, same old. Trying to figure out how to fit in better and get to know my boss and my team but no one really talks unless you get them wasted. A little frustrating."

"Ha. You too, Brutus? Same here. Besides Ian, I really can't speak to anyone unless it involves alcohol. And even with Ian, he seems disinterested in work and would rather discuss food and wine."

Joe paused a second and cracked a smile as if he was going to say something satirical but didn't.

"I'm stating the obvious but we just have to change and adapt to fit into the new environment and survive or we're gonna go nuts. You know, like the chameleon that changes its colors," I continued.

"What are some of the things you're doing to adapt?" Joe asked.

"Well, I started formal Japanese lessons in the office and also subscribed to a podcast to listen to lessons while on the train."

"Nice. I'm signing up for lessons too. Part of the lessons would be Japanese cross-cultural communications. They offered it so I said why not? And what else is new?"

"I joined a gym recently too. Just trying to get some exercise."

"Which gym did you join?" Joe asked as the waitress came to take our order. He was excited to hear because he was a big fan of working out.

"A place right next to Citibank in Akasaka called WOW," I said after ordering two of the grilled *saba* dishes that came with steamed white rice.

"Sounds nice and posh. Does it have a spa, a lap pool, a juice and protein shake bar, personal trainers and masseuses on demand, and open 24 hours?" Joe seemed intrigued.

"You would think, but no. WOW simply stands for Work Out World, some American chain, and has very basic equipment and none of the amenities you mentioned."

Joe seemed confused as the two plates of grilled *saba* were placed on our table.

"So why did you join?"

"Because it's a ten-minute walk from the mansion and I just needed to get back to exercising and to blow off some steam."

"Any hotties?" Joe asked a question that he would ask many, many more times in the coming months.

"Interesting you should ask. It's almost all women there, which is fine by me. Someone told me that the *salarīman* are either still in the office or too busy getting trashed at the bar during the time I go there, which is usually around 7 to 7:30 p.m."

"Sounds like you have a high probability of success there, my friend. Any personal trainers or classes?" Joe became more animated.

"Ha, if that's what I'm after. And yes, I signed up for a yoga class, which was a small mistake because I very quickly learned that I couldn't understand a word the instructor was saying. I got some strange looks from the ladies, probably because I was the only man."

"Nice work. You should come join my gym in Roppongi. Good equipment and very nice scenery, guaranteed. Very international crowd," Joe said with a smirk.

"It's fine. It's cheap and close. One thing I discovered is the sports drink they have that I love, called Pocari Sweat."

"The what sweat? Sounds disgusting!"

"Actually, it's nice and refreshing. But the name is exactly why I didn't try it for a couple of weeks. As a marketer, I would never brand a sports drink with the word 'sweat' in it. It's almost like saying your drink contains sweat."

I couldn't help to revert to talking shop. I could only imagine that the brand manager didn't do proper market research before coming up with that English name.

"I'm no branding expert but they could drop 'sweat' and just call it Pocari. It's almost like Bacardi, but without the rum." Joe now sounded like a marketer.

"I like where you're going with that. Exactly what I would do. I also like 'Aquarius,' made by the Coca Cola Company. Not quite as sweet and it's American, which I try to support as much as possible."

The iconic American firm has a much broader range of product offerings in Japan than they do back home, including at that time a line of coffee drinks called Rainier, a variety of bottled teas, water, and of course Coke Classic. The joke was that for a while, Coke was launching a new product just about every month in Japan because they didn't know what would stick as the market is entirely different. At one point there was a drink called "Salad Water" and you would be right if you guessed that it bombed.

We sat quietly for a while to finish our lunch, all that in less than 15 minutes. We were both well-trained by then to eat super-fast. We got up and walked around the block while chatting, headed for a popular coffee joint called Tully's.

"It sounds like you're not making friends and influencing people in your office either?" I asked Joe as I ordered a cappuccino.

"Well we're in the early innings. Let's give it a chance. My direct report told me this morning that 'The nail that sticks up gets hammered.' Now I get why he's so afraid to speak up in meetings. He's a wild man at the *nomikai* but at the office he's a silent robot."

"I think that's probably because decisions are usually already made behind closed doors and most staff members don't feel that they can make a difference. It's such a hierarchical society."

"True. And how about these late-night teleconferences with the U.S. and people staying in the office until 10, 11 p.m., or later? You do that too?" Joe asked.

"I do it in my mansion. These guys are crazy to stay in the office that late and they rarely see their families. Not my cup of tea."

"Yeah, I think they screw themselves in Japan with this self-sacrifice attitude to accommodate our colleagues in other parts of the world. I think they should ask the Americans to take turns since the Japanese are the bosses." Joe was trying to defend the Japanese, or make it easier for himself, or both.

"I know many of them don't have a home office and it's just easier for them to take calls and to focus in the office. That or they don't care much to see their wives or children, which would be really sad," I added.

"Whatever it is, these late teleconferences at one or two in the morning are getting kind of old. I could never sleep well after talking shop late at night."

"That's why you need to drink more!"

We took a seat outside to drink our Java and to watch the lunch crowd go by.

"Didn't you go back to the U.S. recently?" Joe asked.

"Twice actually, to Philly in late February and to D.C. just last week. Nice experience flying with ANA."

"Yeah, the Japanese take customer service to the next level. I like how they seat you and take your order of food and drinks at the lounge. The warm, moist towel is a nice touch," Joe commented.

"Agree. What impresses me also is that *all* the ladies get up and bow to you with a big smile when you arrive at the reception."

"The Americans have a lot to learn from these folks. I also like how they have a currency exchange machine in the lounge. That's magic."

"For me the best part was the private room the size of a studio apartment built in traditional Japanese style, complete with wood and rice paper sliding doors. There's a *tatami* bed where nursing mothers can go and have some privacy with their babies. I discovered it by accident."

"Did you pop a sleeping pill or how did you cope with that long flight back?"

"No pills and that was a bad rookie mistake. For the trip to Philly, I ended up watching two and a half movies, had a fancy four-course meal with a couple of glasses of Burgundy, and I realized I still had about nine hours to go. So, I pulled out the laptop to try to work but had a massive headache."

Joe raised his eyebrows and shook his head.

"Trust me on this one, next time take an Ambien or drink a lot. It works for me. Don't do any work unless you have to. You need your rest on the plane." Joe had made this journey a few more times than I had.

The other rookie mistakes on that virgin voyage back to the U.S. included scheduling a meeting the same day I arrived. I had no sleep on the plane and every cell in my body ached. Throughout the session I felt like I was having a seizure and could pass out at any moment. Through some inexplicable willpower, I managed to stay composed and awake and I finished the late afternoon meeting without having to be carried away on a stretcher to the emergency room. I was glad to be back to the U.S. of A. although we strangely ended up having Asian food that night at a place called Buddakan and I ordered sushi. I then proceeded to make meaningful contributions to a "competitive simulation" in the next two days where roughly 40 colleagues got in a room and attempted to predict what our competitors would do to us and we devised a contingency and mitigation plan to address those potential threats. I also started to have a bit of an identity crisis because I felt quite happy to be in Japan although not fitting in just yet, and I didn't miss New Jersey except for Renee.

"So, the other unusual thing was I felt like a foreigner being in the U.S. and it's only been three months." I shared this strange emotion with Joe.

"Dude, did you turn Japanese already? I know you're trying hard to assimilate and everything."

"Well I've been studying Japanese a lot, both the language and their culture. And I think I'm also spending a lot more time with Europeans and other non-American colleagues. Probably just part of the natural progression of a global job." I was trying to make some sense out of the way I felt.

"And what about the D.C. trip? You did better on the plane this time I hope?"

"This time I got smart and took a sleeping pill after a glass of the bubblies and only a half glass of chardonnay. The combination knocked me out for at least three to four hours and I was in much better shape than the first trip."

"What did you do in D.C.?" Joe asked.

"Brand planning stuff. It was useful but intense and tiring. The most exciting part was when Ian got into a bizarre 'your mama is so ugly' competition with a colleague after many rounds of vino and subsequently crashed into the glass door on the way out of a restaurant. He had a black eye for about four days. He of course pretended nothing had happened and no one asked."

"Hahaha. Nice story. Sounds like your boss definitely turned Japanese. Let's take a walk and head back. Any big plans for the weekend?"

"Not yet, planning to stick around. You?"

"Why don't you join my co-worker and me in Roppongi to cause some trouble?"

Walking back to my office building, I remembered the questions that my U.S. colleagues asked me while in Washington D.C. They were curious about what it was like to live and work in Japan and whether I missed home. My response was that it was an amazing experience so far but the truth was it was too early to tell. I did feel that I was living in a "bubble" of some sort because many fellow Americans living in Japan, whether it's the English teachers or military personnel, don't get the expat package. I was starting to feel spoiled by the special treatment that I received in the office, the first-class lounges when I traveled, and the extra cash that was accumulating because of the company subsidies. My sense of career progression was becoming blurry as I was getting lost in the euphoria of the good life.

Episode 12 (Jūni): The Roppongi Experiment

"What are you up to?" I Skyped Renee to catch up before heading out to meet Joe and his co-worker one Friday evening.

"School papers and grocery shopping today. How about you?"

"Meeting up with Joe and his friend in Roppongi."

"Sounds like trouble. What's new this week? Besides the Japanese Finance Minister at the G-7 Summit in Rome looking drunk on TV?"

"Yeah, he was a real class act. He had to resign. You don't get to make a fool of yourself on an important world stage like this and keep your job."

"It's just dumb. I mean we're in the middle of a global financial crisis and unemployment is out of control, and instead of discussing solutions to fix the economy, he got hammered."

"Well, he was a bit of scapegoat too I think because Japan has had very high unemployment; over 4 percent which was 1 percent higher than the average of 3 percent in the preceding years."

"That's super low compared to U.S. I mean we're more than double that here."

"Different country, different policies. This figure would have been much higher if you take away the people hired to do seemingly unnecessary and meaningless activities. For example, there are way too many of these men on train and subway station platforms whose only job is to stand around with their microphone and say things like '*Doa ga shimarimas, ashi moto ni gochūi kudasai.*' (The train doors are closing, please be careful and watch your feet.) Thank you, Sherlock, for the warning."

"That's an easy one. How about all those cleaning ladies, always in the public bathrooms? I mean I know they're obsessed with cleanliness but it's a bit much to see them all the time everywhere."

"Oh yeah. Those cleaning ladies in our office building give our bathrooms a total makeover each hour of the day. I'm sure that the bathroom floors in my office building are cleaner than our kitchen counter. What makes me uncomfortable is that they go in the men's room whether there's someone in there or not and irrespective of what the men are doing."

"Speaking from experience?" Renee asked.

"I was both horrified and amused the first time a cleaning lady came in while I was in the midst of a very long piss into the urinal. I'd been in a meeting and held for too long and my pelvic muscles couldn't stop the gush. She acknowledged me and simply said '*sumimasen*' (excuse me) and went on spraying and wiping everything down around me although the place was already spotless."

"Well at least you have clean bathrooms all the time, not like New York City public bathrooms which are disgusting." Renee focused on the positives. "I also think they have way more taxis than needed."

"I think you're right. If I had to guess, I would say that there were probably enough per family and for every drunken person on the streets after the metro shuts down promptly after midnight. In our area almost 100 percent of the cars on the streets after midnight are taxicabs."

"At least you know you can get one and in a color besides yellow and that they're very safe. And you don't have to tip like the U.S."

Renee remembered well the taxis and was particularly impressed by the automatic door that opens in the rear left that's controlled by the driver with a lever. It's convenient when it pours, when you are carrying things, and when people are too drunk to find the door handle. Many drivers are dressed in a suit, wear Mickey Mouse gloves, and are usually very polite. Every car has GPS because the street address system is so convoluted in Tokyo that even the cab drivers can't find where you want to go without consulting the device most of the time. Except for major streets and highways, roads don't have names in Tokyo and directions are given by referencing key landmarks, hotels, train stations, etc. A typical address will include the name of the *ku* (ward or city), number of the *chome* (district), followed by the number of the *ban* (sub-district), and then the *gō* (number) of the building. I wasn't certain how a country that's super modern and advanced in technology and progressive in their thinking had an address system that was archaic and unpractical.

"My favorite example of excess Japanese workers is probably all those guys in hard hats in front of our apartment when they dug up a small hole to put down some new cables. There must have been 15 workers around the site and many of them just standing around to supervise," Renee chimed in.

"It's typical here. You really need only three or four for the job — one operating the Bobcat machine, one directing traffic, and one making sure there are signs around the worksite saying something like 'We are not responsible for any injuries. If you are stupid enough to get too close and get hurt, then it's your fault.' You know those damn lawyers." I couldn't resist.

"Very funny. But seriously, they probably need some massive policy change to improve things. Are there going to be more problems with the economy and more people resigning? They're famous for self-blame and taking accountability by quitting their posts, right?"

"Well, the prime minister, appropriately named Aso, just set new records by having his approval rating in the single digits, making George W. Bush look like a superstar. I don't think he'll last long."

"It's the economy. You fix the economy and everyone is happy I guess," Renee said.

Japan is no different from many countries around the world

where many politicians are legacies of their prior generations. Quite often the prime minister's grandpa or daddy or another relative was also prime minister or president or another high-level government official. I did feel it was much less democratic than, say, the U.S., where at least you have to go through a much more complicated election process from state primaries to the Electoral College, popular votes, etc. I didn't think someone like Obama, who was virtually unknown with the general public just a few years ago before he became president, would have had a chance in the political scene in Japan, although I could be wrong. The men at the highest level of government there (virtually no women) all went to the same two or three schools (Tokyo University being the most common) and had known each other all their lives because their parents or grandparents also knew each other.

⛩

Roppongi was an expat heaven in terms of shopping, non-stop entertainment, and everything else a *gaijin* would need. When the American military occupied Japan for seven years after the Second World War in 1945, the GIs turned this area into their favorite hangout and took some of the prime real estate and built the U.S. Embassy and a massive living compound. It was a rather posh area with two of Japan's tallest buildings both about a 10- to 15-minute walk from my flat. At the time, Roppongi Hills had over 200 upscale shops and restaurants, bars, and residences. Its rival, the Tokyo Midtown Tower, had dozens of high-end shops and restaurants and was right next to a Ritz-Carlton and a couple of ultra-luxurious condos for the super-rich. You knew you were in a league of your own when you were living in Roppongi Hills because a 600 square foot studio apartment would set you back $10,000 a month. Joe lived in such an apartment. The same age as me, he worked hard during the day and partied even harder at night. A single, handsome, and well-to-do man, he was a perfect formula for trouble in Tokyo where trouble was just one step away.

. . .

I strolled over to Joe's mansion after my Skype session with Renee and it took just 15 minutes. Joe's friend had changed his plan and couldn't join us, so we each drank a can of Ebisu Premium Malts quickly and hit the streets of Roppongi. The most curious thing for me in Roppongi was the large African presence in this neighborhood. They weren't Americans, because of their accent, and I didn't think they made a good living hawking the various adult entertainment establishments on the streets. They would always spot Joe a kilometer away and try to "help" him with his needs.

"Excuse me, sir, would you like to meet beautiful Japanese women?" a tall African of unknown origin said to Joe.

"No thanks, we're meeting some friends," Joe responded without looking at him and kept walking. I was completely ignored.

Most of these guys assumed that I was Japanese and Joe's interpreter and wouldn't even speak to me. Joe has striking, chiseled features and a shaved head and can pass for a Middle-Easterner, an Italian, or Greek (or other variants from the Mediterranean), a Native American, an African-American, or a Latin-American. Surprisingly he's an East Indian born in New Delhi but grew up in the States. His name could have been Faizal, Rahul, Ahmed, Carlos, Jerome, Nikolas, Mario, or Dances with Wolves. But instead it's a generic Joe. Half a dozen more African dudes harassed Joe, some followed and touched him to persuade him to visit their establishment to have "the night of his life." It got a little aggressive and we decided to run inside a crowded British pub to get away for a while.

"Man, the pressure to buy was intense. It's obvious these guys hadn't taken the Zig Ziglar course on successful selling," I said after I got inside this seemingly popular pub call the First Bar.

Before we could proceed further, we saw a young Caucasian woman stumbling and passing out on the ground right in front of us. A good sign. It certainly wasn't the "first" bar in Tokyo but it was probably the largest (so they claimed). The pub was British by birth, with Guinness and Newcastle on tap and billiards and darts in the back room, but the crowd was anything but British. We stood there feeling a bit bewildered and amused, trying to figure out a game plan.

"Beer," Joe said as he stared at the VIP section where a well-dressed Russian mob stood with their token "models" in skintight black dresses that barely covered their behinds. They were drowning themselves in bottles of Veuve Clicquot and looking very important.

I wasn't sure if it was a question or a statement from Joe. I walked up to the bar and ordered two Guinnesses.

"Cheers, brother. You should also check out the Yakuza dudes in their fitted suits and ties in their sunglasses under the big TV showing Premier League soccer," I said to Joe as I gave him his Irish stout.

"Looks like they're smoking Virginia Slims. Wusses. Probably from their expressionless lady companions. Didn't know skinny cigarettes are in fashion," Joe chuckled.

"And how about these three guys being surrounded by twice as many Japanese girls? Am I missing something?" That got Joe's attention.

In the middle of a small dance floor, we saw a mixture of French-speaking male students or teachers in their jeans and sneakers gyrating around their newly found Japanese lady friends who were all too happy to comply.

"I'm too old for this shit," I said to Joe as I surveyed the room further.

"Me too, but we're in Tokyo on a Friday night. Let's get pissed."

"Weren't you an English teacher somewhere?" I asked Joe.

"No, but seeing this action I wish I was."

We stared some more while taking a big gulp of the Guinness. Like two misfits who weren't quite sure what the hell was going on, we ended up playing darts and had another Guinness while trying to revise the game plan for the evening.

"What time is it?" I asked.

"8:30."

"Let's blow this popsicle stand. It's dead anyway."

We walked 50 meters and visited Vibrations, a small underground club where about half the patrons were Africans and most were probably half our age.

"Why are we here again?" I asked Joe.

"I'm supposed to meet a girl I met a few nights ago. I remember what she looks like but I forget her name," Joe explained.

"That's very brave of you, and funny."

"It'll come back to me. Do me a favor and introduce yourself when I give you the signal," Joe instructed.

"No problem; happy to be wingman."

While we waited, a convoy of ladies entered the club and struck up a conversation with Joe.

"So, you're Americans too?" Joe asked.

"Nooooo, Canadians! We're entertainers from Saskatchewan."

"So, when you said you're 'entertainers,' d'you mean you're exotic dancers?" Joe was very direct.

"Oh, we're not strippers!" one of them stated unprompted, which meant they definitely were.

We quickly noticed an African dude accompanied them; seemed to be the theme of the evening. Friendly ladies and very intoxicated. After nearly losing our hearing and our voice talking to these Canadian entertainers, we bailed to get a bite to eat. Joe's mysterious friend never showed up. Or perhaps she did but Joe couldn't recognize her.

I broke my own rule and grabbed a burger at Mickey D's around the corner to neutralize the already high alcohol content in my bloodstream.

First burger in Japan in three months. Joe refused to give in to eating American food and we chatted for a while and then went for a stroll to look for the next spot. After freestyling for a while on the streets and getting tired of being bombarded by Nigerians, we stumbled upon a nice café, darted in, and took a shot of caffeine to catch our second wind. We found our next and final venue for the evening, a club called Muse, one of the coolest places I'd been so far in Tokyo — massive and underground, with several themed rooms, nooks, karaoke lounges, billiards, a blackjack table, and a VIP room. I was about 15 years too old for that place. As in many other clubs around Tokyo, there were lockers for storing important personal belongings, very thoughtful.

"I like this place; it's mostly Japanese," Joe observed.

"Never mind that we're too old; it's a cool spot."

"Who cares? We're *gaijin* and having fun. Besides, it makes me feel young. Drink?" Joe could keep going all night.

"No, I think I'll pass. Let me get you a drink?"

We parted ways eventually as I was falling asleep in the Muse and I stumbled home. Joe went on infusing his body with other potions and looking for his personal muse. According to his recollection later, he went back to Vibrations and met up with his alleged lady friend. Unfortunately for him he passed out after having drunk spiked drinks and woke up about 7 a.m. on a couch in a different bar. The lady and her friends were long gone and so were his wallet and credit cards.

Episode 13 (Jūsan): The American Doctor

"How was your trip to Orlando? Anything interesting to report?" Renee asked on my return from business meetings in the U.S.

"Trip was good. I was busy attending scientific sessions and schmoozing some important cardiologists over nice dinners and fine wine. You know, just doing the job," I said.

"Sounds better than reading 100 pages of contract law. Did you see some friends from the U.S. office?"

"Yep, had dinner with former colleagues from Jersey and celebrated a birthday with a couple of bottles of nice champagne while catching up on company gossip. Nothing crazy."

"Sounds good. Did Ian join you?"

"He wasn't always with me but he had strict orders that the global team must always pay for all dinners involving customers and affiliates. He said the big boss isn't happy if we don't spend money treating our key stakeholders."

"Sounds rough! What's your limit?" Renee asked innocently.

"He said he'll let me know if my expenses are excessive. He also told me that no one has ever questioned his spending in the past ten years."

"I hate you."

The guidance was of course music to my ears. Nevertheless, I was careful and reasonable. My dinners were indeed quite "proper," I thought, but apparently I didn't even come close to the limit as I found out later when submitting my expense report. Obviously, I had a lot to learn as *gaijin* number two.

Going to dinner with Ian was a lesson in fine dining. A typical meal usually started with a beer (naturally) while he inspected the wine list. He would then order a modestly-priced California chardonnay, usually from the Sonoma or Napa Valley, as warm-up. Inevitably he would select a near-luxury Burgundy as we got to the main course, something less than $100. He would always carefully examine the wine by sniffing the cork and do his swirling of the glass and a quick pressure-test by swishing the liquid in his mouth to make sure the wine's integrity and quality hadn't been altered. The appetizers and main course were ordered to complement the wine and not the other way around.

"Surely there must have been a good story from last week?" Renee's probing continued.

"Well, the most entertaining part was probably the night before we left Orlando when we had a very nice meal," I said.

"A nice steak and some good French wine?"

"Not just any steak. Ono-san ordered a $100 Kobe beef steak which made Ian flinch a bit but he let it go."

"That's very generous of Ian."

"We had a good week. Ian wanted to celebrate. None of us objected. Ono-san's a special guy, a *Tōdai* (Tokyo University, best in Japan) graduate and a sommelier in training. He ordered the whole meal for us."

"Wow! That's cool. So you could just sit back and relax."

"Yeah, it's well-accepted that Ono is the heir apparent to Ian as the wine expert at all company dinners."

"Sounds like a good career move on his part and a dream job for you — getting experience in global marketing and real-world training in fine wine and haute cuisine." Renee couldn't have said it better. "So that's it? What's the scandalous or controversial part?"

"Well there were a couple of things. Ono brought a special guest on the trip and Ian sent back a couple of $100 bottles of wine saying the cork was bad."

"Ono brought his wife?"

"No, that wouldn't be special. He brought a girlfriend."

"What?"

"Well Ian and I both thought he was married with a teenage daughter but it was none of our business and we didn't question further."

"OK, so maybe he's recently divorced or separated. And the bad cork?"

"I've never seen anything like it. When the server brought out the first bottle of the Burgundy Grand Cru, Ian took a long sip, had a concerned look on his face, and examined the cork. He then told the waiter to open a new bottle because the wine had gone bad."

"And what happened?"

"The waiter was hesitant and so he called the sommelier. The sommelier came, looked at the cork and sniffed it, and confirmed the cork was indeed damaged and the content inside had morphed into something unrecognizable. They opened a new bottle."

"You said two bottles?"

"Yes, Ian thought the second bottle was bad too and asked them to open a third bottle. Which they did. I was amazed how calm everyone was. After that, no more drama. But it was tense for a few minutes. I was impressed by how the restaurant handled the whole situation, and so was Ian. We had a lovely meal and left a big tip. And what's new and exciting on your end?" I asked Renee.

"Not much really. School and more school, just waiting for the semester to be over. Wish I was having a nice Kobe steak and drinking fancy French wine. You have the life that most people would envy."

"It's only a job. But yeah, I can't complain."

"Don't take it for granted because before you know it, your assignment will be over and you'll be back to living a life like us commoners."

"You're such a party-pooper. It's only started. The worst part of the trip was the damage it did to my back though." I went on to tell Renee the whole sorry saga.

The trip to Florida had mostly been uneventful except it compelled me to pay a visit to a Japanese emergency room on my return to Tokyo. Between the jet lag, all the hours standing around and attending sessions at the congress, I'd aggravated my chronic bad back and I was desperate for a quick fix before I got on the return flight. A colleague gave me a Vicodin, an opioid-based painkiller, and I washed it down with a glass of wine. That night I saw angels while riding a dragon flying through Disney World and I was going so fast it made my head spin and everything became very blurry. I woke up with a tremendous headache and on the way back to Tokyo my back was so stiff I could've bounced a coin off it. The pain was so intense, I ordered a bucket of ice from the cabin attendant so I could ice my back down throughout most of the 14-hour trip.

The lesson from the Florida trip: don't mix alcohol with Vicodin.

After returning to Tokyo, I took a couple of days off as I couldn't stand up straight after getting off the airplane. After being bedridden for 24 hours, I decided I needed to see a healthcare professional. I got a copy of the weekly English circular *Metropolis* and found an American doctor called Shane at the appropriately named Shane Clinic (some called it the Tokyo American Clinic) which was in Roppongi. I was a bit skeptical because the ad said this physician had been practicing since right after the Second World War and he was still in practice. Assuming he was a child prodigy and finished medical school as a teenager and started practicing Doogie Howser style immediately, he had to be close to 80 years old. He sounded like an extremely experienced practitioner and I was desperate and didn't know enough Japanese yet to venture into a hospital emergency room.

"*Moshi moshi* (hello), my name's Marcus and I would like to make an appointment with Dr. Shane for my bad back," I said over the phone.

"This is Shane. My schedule is wide open and I can take you in the next hour if you can come in now," replied a gentle and clear voice on the other end.

That was too easy, I thought. I got up from the bed and baby-stepped to the closest metro station from my mansion, one limp at a time, and headed for his clinic. Dr. Shane was a gentle man with a full head of white hair and stood about 157 centimeters with shoes on. He was definitely an octogenarian and his office was like a time capsule with a setup that probably hadn't changed much since WWII. I thought I'd walked into a museum instead of a working clinic and I wondered if I'd come to the right place. It was charming and even nostalgic and I felt like I was on the set of *M.A.S.H.*, the popular TV show from the '70s and '80s about the Korean War. There were black and white pictures of post-war Japan in the '40s and '50s on the wall, a full-size plastic skeleton, and old-fashioned equipment and diagnostic tools from a bygone era. After some initial dialogue about my issues, I got on the military-style exam bed and Shane took my pulse, did some manipulations on my legs, and tapped my knees to make sure they flexed. He made notes, asked me some more questions, and pondered for a second.

"You have lower back spasm due to herniated discs on your spinal column," he announced confidently.

"That sounds serious. Do I need surgery?"

"Don't worry; it's nothing. Just take some good painkillers and stretch a lot. You'll be fine."

"That's it? Are you sure?" I exclaimed, not completely convinced. "Don't I have a pinched nerve or a fracture or something else?"

"I don't think so, young man. No need to stress. I've seen thousands of patients like you with the same problem. Now go across the street to the Mita hospital and get a scan just to make sure," Shane instructed.

"But I don't know enough Japanese."

"You don't need to. I'm going to write you a note. You'll give it to them and they'll know what to do. We'll chat again when I get the results."

"Could you at least give me some morphine, you know, for the pain?"

"You watch too many movies, young man. I haven't done that since the Korean War. I'll give you muscle relaxer and a good painkiller called Loxonin; that will take care of it."

I paused and felt a bit foolish asking for morphine. I was still thinking about *M.A.S.H.* I didn't want to question the good doctor but I thought the diagnosis and prognosis were all a bit too simple and I briefly considered getting a second opinion. Ironically the effective painkiller was made and marketed by my Japanese employer at the time.

"Any other issues or physical illness I can help you with?" asked the amicable Dr. Shane.

"I think I'm good for now, sir. Thank you for taking care of me today, sir." I said, after slowly getting up from his metal-frame bed and seeing more photos of American soldiers in uniform on the wall.

I was in no shape to try to find another doc so I waddled slowly and reluctantly across the street like an injured penguin to the Mita hospital to get a set of x-ray and MRI. The whole point of going to see Shane was to avoid a trip to the ER where I might not fare so well because of the language issues. On the way to the hospital, I had a flashback to 1996, the only time I'd been to an ER. I was struck by a taxi while on rollerblades in Santa Monica, California. I ended up spending five days in the hospital and incurred a $20,000 medical bill. It was an experience I'd rather forget. I hobbled to the reception, gave them the note from Dr. Shane, hoping it would be a quick in-and-out and no-hospital stay. Ultimately, with my rudimentary Japanese, their high school English, plus some impromptu sign language, they understood that I had a back problem requiring x-ray and MRI for further diagnosis. With the help of the dictionary in my flip phone, I was able to fill out a super lengthy and complex medical history chart in Japanese.

I paid the customary 30 percent co-pay for Japanese nationals (my company had provided me with local government insurance) and proceeded to a room where they strapped me to a table like a prisoner and rotated it around to take some radiographic pictures. I waited a bit longer to have the MRIs taken and ended up spending at least a couple of hours more at the hospital before hailing a cab to get home. And with that I'd successfully navigated through a Japanese hospital. I was in no hurry to do it again.

From that experience I learned that most Japanese people typically don't go to see a primary care physician as we do in the U.S. In fact, they usually don't have a family doctor. They'll go to the hospital if they're really ill to get a prescription for meds. I also thought the two hours in the ER wasn't bad at all compared to my previous experience in an American emergency room where I waited five to six hours to be seen despite having been struck by a car. In the U.S., I was competing with folks who were shot by a gun or suffering from other life-threating injuries or symptoms.

Episode 14 (Jūyon): Underneath the Sakura

In a two-week span, between late March and early April, the streets of Tokyo turn into a light shade of pink. It is *hanami* (flower-viewing) season. The *sakura* (cherry blossoms) transform the cityscape during this fortnight to usher in spring. It's one of the most stunning sights that accompany the change of season; one which Japanese and foreigners alike take time to admire and appreciate. I was looking forward to my first proper *hanami*.

"Murayama-san, what's the plan for *hanami*?"

Caught by surprise, Murayama-san looked up slowly, pointed her forefinger at her nose, and had a puzzled look.

"You know, the *sakura*-viewing party," I went on. "Since you're the organizer of the department, I thought you'd have a plan for us?" I said halfway seriously.

"You like the *sakura*?"

I nodded. "Yes, I read a lot about the custom of *hanami*. I like the Japanese tradition of folks gathering, usually with some sake, to admire the beauty of the *sakura* while socializing with family, friends, and co-workers."

"Wow, I'm impressed. Do you do *hanami* in the U.S.?"

"Well, some, but it's not the same. There are cherry trees in

America of course, and they're equally beautiful, but I think there's a much greater significance and meaning for the Japanese people."

I was thinking that Americans would get arrested for getting wasted in a park.

"Well, I haven't planned anything but I suppose I could if everyone is interested."

She looked around the team and a few other people nodded also.

"OK, let me do something."

And just like that, Murayama-san, the U.K.-educated MBA in my department, volunteered to organize an excursion after my initial inquiry. In many corporations, including the one I worked for in Japan, the class of new hires is usually in charge of scoping out a venue (usually a park) where a department can get together and sit on a plastic tarp to have a snack with some beer, preferably directly under a cherry tree. The festivity can last hours as they take the chance to get away from the office and officially usher in warmer weather. I was excited and really looking forward to the outing later that week.

Less than half an hour later, Murayama-san had a plan.

"We are going to Kitanomaru Kōen. It was once part of the Imperial Palace built during the Edo era (1600-1868). You are going to like it."

We left work early on a Friday afternoon to get on the metro and found ourselves surrounded by thousands of *sakura* spectators with the same plan who had already packed the place by the time the eight of us arrived around 5:45 p.m. It was quite a spectacle.

My colleague Ono-san, an expert in just about every subject matter, said, "You know, Chen-san, all cherry trees are cloned; that's why they all bloom at the same time."

"No kidding. I didn't know they could do that. Is that how the Japanese also figured out how to clone sheep later?"

There was a bit of sarcasm there but Ono didn't quite get it and just nodded politely.

"Well, the *sakura* is stunning but it is short-lived. It is like the

Japanese people where most have brief moments of brilliance and glory but then they quickly fade away," he told me.

"Ono-san, that's beautiful and sad. Are you also a poet?"

"Yes. I mean no. It is my own analogy. Yes."

He looked confused and nodded again. He had more to say. "There are more than 100 species of sakura but they all seem to have a light pink hue, more off-white actually. Please enjoy." He then took out his flip phone and started taking pictures. A signal that our conversation was over for now.

I didn't understand why we got there so late then I noticed that they'd lit up the park and shined the lights on the trees to give the gorgeous blossoms a pinker color. The scenery was truly magnificent with thousands of cherry trees, many of them centuries-old, blooming at once against the backdrop of the impressive and elegant Imperial Palace grounds. The bursts of pink *sakura* provided a stark contrast to the calm, gray background in the park that included a moat surrounding the palatial grounds.

I must have heard the word "*kirei*" (pretty) a thousand times as we walked through the park. Typically a reticent, reserved bunch, the Japanese couldn't hide their admiration and appreciation for these millions of pink flowers that dominated the scenery. Occasionally a light breeze came through and countless petals would fall, swirl, seemingly in slow motion and resembling a *sakura* storm, landing on the *sakura*-gazers' clothes, hair, and sometimes gently hitting the face. I grabbed the petals that landed on my face and tried to smell them. The scent was ever so subtle but with a detectable fragrance that was lightly sweet with a hint of cherry fruit.

I felt like I was part of a picture-perfect cover shot from *National Geographic* underneath all the *sakura*. I stood still for a long moment to admire the spectacular setting and I felt the energy emitting from the splendid surroundings. It was another one of those incredible experiences you can only obtain by being in Japan. Everyone on my team was now focusing on taking close-up pictures with 4G NTT Docomo flip phones. Nobody spoke for a long while as we inched at snail-pace along a narrow walkway. Hundreds of men in uniform performed traffic and crowd control.

We pushed through the crowd and crossed the street to Yasukuni Shrine, a famous but extremely controversial park and one of Tokyo's grandest shrines conceived by Emperor Meiji which houses about two and a half million war dead and several WWII generals. Depending on whom you talk to, these military leaders enshrined there were considered war criminals or heroes.

Not wanting to get into an uncomfortable conversation, I turned my attention to food.

"So, should we get some food and drinks?" I asked Murayama-san.

"Of course, we can stop and get some *yakimono* (grilled foods) from any one of these street vendors. There must be hundreds of them. Unfortunately there's no place to sit."

"I see. I'm definitely going to get a *yaki*-something. And a beer."

I recruited Ono-san and we each had some grilled squid, Osaka style. It was fantastic. Others on my team considered but took no action.

"We should go to a restaurant to have a proper dinner," said Murayama-san. Everyone agreed.

I looked around and realized that every centimeter of that park was occupied with folks sitting on plastic sheets, eating and boozing away, some singing, some passed out, all with their shoes off and neatly placed and lined up at the edge of the plastic tarp. What an orderly group of people.

"Don't tell me we're going to Denny's?" I said to Murayama incredulously as we arrived at the American restaurant later that evening.

"Unfortunately every place I called is booked and this is the only option if we want to eat."

"Seriously, everything's full? Wow!" I was disappointed and felt silly going to a Denny's, which I wouldn't normally go to in the U.S.

"I think some pitchers of Kirin will make it better for you, Chen-san," said Nobu-san.

And drink we did, in record time I would add, to quench our thirst. There were no major scandals to report as the two female colleagues, including the event organizer, Murayama, had to attend a teleconference at 9 p.m. and had to leave early to return to the office.

"Seriously? Only a Friday night? After *hanami*?" I asked incredulously.

They nodded quietly and gathered their things and headed back to the office. Surprising and sad. I reckoned the bosses were either completely oblivious to the personal time that employees might want to have after hours or they chose to ignore it completely. In any event I respected the local business practice but didn't quite share this sacrificial spirit and I did everything I could to keep my Friday nights free.

Episode 15 (Jūgo): Japanese Lessons

I believe you can't fully experience a culture without learning its language if you're to stay long term in a foreign country. Of course, having an open mind and a sense of adventure and curiosity are also prerequisites for you to truly appreciate what a country has to offer. Expats have different philosophies about devoting time to learning a foreign language, especially if the time is short or if it's a language you're not likely to ever use again. For me it was simple:

1. I had a personal interest and I liked the way Japanese sounds.
2. I worked for a Japanese company and I wanted to connect better with my bosses and colleagues and also know what people said around me at work.
3. I was going to be in Japan for three years and I wasn't going to leave without at least being quite conversant.

Since late February that year, I'd had one-on-one lessons twice a week. My self-taught *Rosetta Stone* course was good enough to order *ramen* and a beer in a restaurant but to make sense of life in Japan, I needed to improve at my eighth language pronto.

"Like many European languages, there is the formal (or polite) and the informal, casual words and phrases that one uses depending on who one is with." Miyagi Sensei, a lady in her 30s, began my first lesson with this introduction; facts that I knew already.

I wanted to be polite so I nodded slowly and let her continue.

"It can get very confusing at first as there are so many ways to say the same thing. For example, there are probably ten variations of 'I'm sorry,' from the casual '*gomen*,' to the very serious '*mōshiwake arimasen*' which one would only use in the most severe circumstance."

You don't say. I knew that too but she was on a roll so I let it go.

"No one ever wants to say the word 'no' in Japanese. It's as if it is a sin and you go to jail for it. Instead people have all these polite, convoluted ways of avoiding it and hoping that you just go away or 'get the message.' Expressions like '*chotto*,' or '*etto*,' '*muzukashī*,' or '*sō desu ne...*'"

Miyagi Sensei had this speech memorized it seemed but did it very well and it was useful for a beginner for sure. The whole time she was talking, all I could think about was *The Karate Kid*, where Mr. Miyagi transformed a young Ralph Macchio from a bullying target to a martial arts sensation whose signature crane-kick was then imitated by kids across America for many years.

"Everything is 'high context' in Japan and one must learn how to 'read the air,' so to speak, in just about every situation as people try to use as few words as possible."

"I've already experienced that in real life, having read about it before I came to Japan. It's something I'm having a hard time getting used to," I said to Migayi.

"There's even a word that describes someone who's unable to read the air; we say 'KY,'" Migayi Sensei explained further. "If someone is KY, which stands for '*kūki o yomenai*' (cannot read air), that person isn't going to do well in corporate Japan as he or she will inevitably make blunders and get knocked down and probably have to look for another job constantly."

"Oh. Sounds serious."

"And you probably know already that there are three writing systems — kanji, which is Chinese characters; hiragana, the traditional Japanese alphabet; and katakana, a writing system used for all words with foreign origin."

"That I do know, yes. I was impatient, so I've already memorized the hiragana and katakana characters."

"That's very good. You are proactive. I have a feeling you are going to be a very good student, an easy one for me." Miyagi-san complimented me and went on.

"So, to be able to read the newspaper, one needs to memorize about 2,000 different kanji characters and know their meanings. Unlike Korea, who also adopted its writing system from the Chinese two millennia ago but has since created its own writing system and mostly abandoned the Chinese words, Japan has kept much of the kanji in its writing system."

"Wow. You're a linguist and a historian. I kind of cheated because I know Mandarin already so I understand just about all the kanji I see in the Japanese," I replied.

"Well then, I think my job is halfway done here." Miyagi sat back and smiled.

"Not quite. I'm very confused with the *hatsuon* (pronunciation) and the *bunpō* (grammar); both seem very tricky to me. I mean, the same Chinese character can have three, four, or five different ways of pronouncing it. And then I see that in a typical phrase, there can be kanji, katakana, and hiragana all in the same sentence. Very strange."

"Ah, that's the beauty of *Nihongo* (Japanese language). We have to do something original, right?" Miyagi said with pride.

"I guess. I do like it, don't get me wrong, as long as I can understand it. Now, on the grammar, what's the secret of mastering it? It appears that every sentence ends in a verb."

"True. In English you say, 'I am eating sushi.' In Japanese, you say, '*Sushi o taberu.*' Which is 1) sushi, 2) object-marking particle, 3) eat."

"*Omoshiroi* (interesting)," I said.

"One usually figures out who the 'subject' is based on the context of the sentence. Therefore, we also omit many of the subjects and pronouns, just to make it more confusing for foreigners. To us, it is implied."

There are many other unusual rules but suffice it to say that life began to make a lot more sense, and was overall more enjoyable, after I began the twice-weekly lessons with Miss Miyagi.

Unlike her namesake Mr. Miyagi in *The Karate Kid*, she didn't know karate.

Ian, who went through a similar ritual a few years back when he first came to Japan, also recommended *japanesepod101.com*. It's a subscription-based, virtual language school where you can download podcasts and do exercises online. I found it to be particularly practical since I spent about an hour each day on the train commuting during the week. From the podcasts I learned slang and informal expressions that are used more frequently in everyday usage that I didn't get from my formal lessons; a good complement. The program was started by a guy from New York who was a student and an English teacher in Japan and I thought the curriculum and the teaching approach were innovative.

They had a great cast of actors and the dialogues in the lessons were often quite comical in the laugh-out-loud kind of way. One night I tried a common Japanese expression on my colleagues and over-emphasized the intonations and they were laughing so hard I thought someone might get hurt. They simply didn't see it coming from *gaijin* number two.

"*Osaki ni shitsurei shimaaaaas* (my apologies for leaving before you)," I said with passion and conviction as I got up from my chair.

Half a dozen colleagues heard it and their eyes bulged and their mouths dropped open. Their expressions were simply priceless. They must have thought I'd become fluent in Japanese overnight.

"*Ooooohhhhh, Chen-san, Nihongo ga jozu desu ne!* (Mr. Chen, your Japanese is really good!)"

The word *jozu* means 'good at' and the Japanese use it to describe a beginner speaker or a fluent speaker and everything in between. Again, another polite way to compliment someone.

"*Iie, iie,*" I said, dismissing it as you should.

Yes, I said the "N" word. This was one occasion where it was OK to say "no" as I waved my hand and headed for the elevator at 5:30 p.m. on the dot.

Episode 16 (Jūroku): Epidemic Strikes

In Japan, the period between late April and early May is called Golden Week, a unique week-long break for students and workers that includes a variety of national holidays. These include an emperor's birthday, Citizen's Day, Children's Day, Greenery Day, and the Constitution Memorial Day. Most companies are shut down during this week. It became known as Golden Week because many entertainment-related industries such as the cinema see a huge boost in revenue during the period as people are off work and look for fun ways to spend time with the family. It's golden for the travel and hospitality industries as well since it's the longest vacation period in the year for the Japanese and bookings are full despite inflated prices. Renee took advantage of my break and came to Tokyo to visit me before her official move toward the end of the year.

"It's great to be back to Tokyo. The weather is so much nicer now, perfect for visiting the Japanese gardens."

"You just missed the *hanami* but plenty of nice things to see and neighborhoods to explore before the rainy season comes in June."

"I know. I definitely want to see Shinjuku Garden. I heard the Japanese garden there is one of the best in Tokyo. Also, I read about

Daikayama and its boutique shops; worth a visit I think." Renee had done her homework and made a plan.

"You have expensive tastes! I know about Daikayama; it's an upscale district next to Shibuya popular with fashionistas roaming its many posh clothing stores. I've been to Shinjuku Garden, with Camille and Duncan and their daughter, Isla, when they made a stop in Tokyo on their way to Australia back in February. Good place to relax for half a day."

"Then it's a plan!"

I'd seen Renee in person only once, in Philadelphia, between January and May that year. Thanks to Skype, it was as if we were together the whole time. We really liked our first trip to Daikayama but were too cheap to purchase anything. We did take mental notes about the charming alleys and earmarked a few choice shops we could visit sometime in the future. We stumbled upon a Mexican restaurant and I suggested that we have lunch there.

"Really, you want to eat Mexican food in Tokyo?" Renee asked sarcastically. She had grown up eating Mexican food in Arizona and wasn't sure if Tokyo was the right place to get Mexican.

"I do because I haven't had Mexican food for a while. It would also be a nice change from the rice and noodles that I've been eating just about every day since I got here."

Having grown up in Texas, Mexican cuisine is something that's nostalgic for me. We took a chance and went to the restaurant where we discovered that the Japanese couple who ran the place had learned to cook Mexican food in Guadalajara, Mexico. We ordered tacos and enchiladas and they were surprisingly authentic and delicious. Feeling satisfied, and a bit homesick, we then headed for the Shinjuku Garden one metro station away.

It was Renee's first visit to Shinjuku Garden, a sanctuary in the city that we would visit many more times during our stay in Japan. This vast garden was meticulously designed and built very much in a central part of Tokyo. It housed a traditional Japanese garden, a well-designed Chinese garden, and a respectable English garden. With an entry fee of about $2.00, it was practically free and a great way to spend an afternoon. We picked up a cup of coffee and sat on the lawn under the *sakura* trees next to a massive koi pond.

"What else do you miss from home besides Mexican food?" Renee asked.

"You know, the ease of going wherever I want, in the car, on a whim, was nice. I would never get lost. Here it's a place I'm still trying to figure out. Simple things like where to get essential supplies without paying ridiculous amounts of money or figuring out how to have a decent conversation with people. It takes time to adjust but I'll get there."

"It's just like that every time we move to a new place. New Jersey isn't quite home for us."

"That's exactly what I feel. Tokyo's just another place on our life's journey. It's a great place with a different language but the feeling was similar when I moved to Chicago, or L.A., or Phoenix, or Connecticut." I reminded myself that I'd moved every two to three years for the past fifteen years.

We both paused to admire the perfectly manicured lawn in the Japanese garden in the middle of the huge metropolis. Four months had passed since I arrived in Japan.

After a relaxing break in the garden, we took a walk around the neighborhood. We quickly stumbled upon a fancy, bordering on extravagant, fruit shop where the price of each piece of fruit was more than $100. Renee stopped in front of square watermelons on display in the store front and had a puzzled look.

"A hundred dollars for these funny looking square watermelons? What's the point of this?" Renee asked, holding a cup of Starbucks coffee in one hand.

"Ah, there's a lot of meaning in these special fruits and one day I'll write about them," I said as a stylishly dressed lady with oversized sunglasses walking her Yorkshire terrier strolled by.

"Why? It's just fruit," Renee said.

"Not just fruit! It's a nice analogy to my expat experiences here so far. The watermelon tastes the same inside, although it looks very different from the outside. So, whether you're an American, or

Japanese, or African, or Latin, or whatever, human beings are pretty much the same inside. But the value that's perceived by others externally, based on how you look or how you present yourself because of the environment in which you grew up, could be very different."

"OK, that concept makes sense to me. But I still don't get why it's square," Renee interrupted before I could finish.

"It's square because the *purpose* is so different. These watermelons aren't only for eating or to quench thirst; they've been grown in square boxes so that they look like a *present* in that boxy shape. Gift-giving is a huge deal in Japan and they've turned an ordinary fruit into an exceptional present," I explained with a business slant.

"I see. You're saying that we have to adapt to a new environment or to serve a different purpose, like having to learn a new skill or language, change our appearance, or adjust our attitude to fit in or even to survive."

"Exactly! And that's a great analogy. Couldn't have said it better. The same object has been modified and is presented differently to fetch a much higher price. I would never pay $100 for a round or an oblong-shaped watermelon. But a square one with a red bow on it? Well that's unique and worth the price."

"I never thought of it as a present. I just think it looks cool, maybe a little bizarre, and that it's easier for the shops to display and stack them up high."

"Ha, that's funny. You took the words out of my mouth. Japanese farmers found an ingenious way to grow them into squares because of limited spaces in people's fridge and precisely because it's easier to store them."

"Well I think it's a good title for a book if you end up writing it. I would buy and read it."

"Thanks for the support. But what's happening here in Japan is quite interesting and it's keeping things fresh for me. Maybe that's why I haven't thought much about home so much. Plus, I'm trying really hard to get acclimated here."

"I heard Japan's economy isn't doing too hot. How does that affect your job?"

Renee was aware of the economic troubles in Japan, like the rest of the world during the Great Recession of 2009, and no major economies of the world were spared.

"Well it's bad everywhere but here we saw the annualized GDP contraction of more than 13 percent, Japan's worst ever. Unemployment hit a historical high of 5 percent, which still seems super low to me compared to the 10 percent we have in the U.S. But to answer your question, I don't think it affects me at all because my position is global and people always need medicine."

"Is the Japanese government providing a stimulus package to encourage spending like they did in the U.S.?"

"They sent out checks worth about $120. Even I, a bona fide *gaijin*, received a deposit of ¥12,000 in my checking account. And because they put cash in people's pockets, Prime Minister Aso's approval rating has skyrocketed to 30 percent, his highest in recent memory."

"What did you do with the money? Just enough to have a nice night out, I guess?" Renee's no fool, knowing that the cost of living is sky-high in Tokyo and $120 seemed like a pittance.

"Exactly. Not as generous as what Uncle Sam gave us but I did celebrate with some new friends that I met through Joe by eating the famous *okonomiyaki*. It's a type of Japanese savory pancake originally from the Kansai region."

"I don't know this one but it sounds like the Korean pancakes with seafood and cabbage?" Renee asked, being a big fan of Korean cuisine.

"Yes. It's not the prettiest thing when it's being prepared and thrown onto the grill. It reminded me of vomit, with the chopped-up cabbage in a white liquid and some small shrimp and bacon on top. But the finished product, with grilled *soba* added on top, is truly *oishī* (delicious)."

"Never judge a dish by its raw ingredients. And that's it? You spent your entire windfall on the pancake?"

"No, there was more. After the *okonomiyaki* tasting, we went to a nightclub in our neighborhood, in the basement of Antwerp Port, a Belgian pub and restaurant."

"I thought you said you're too old for that?"

"I am and I wasn't really into it, until some stranger, an American or Canadian, came up to me at the restaurant and shouted into my ear, 'Hey! Can you smell what The Rock is cooking?' I cracked up hysterically because I remembered people back home had sometimes commented that I look like Dwayne 'The Rock' Johnson. You know, the actor and former pro-wrestler. I decided to hang out with them that night because they seemed like a lot of fun."

"Yeah, I remember. But I certainly think you're better looking and have more hair."

That comment from the English teacher of North American origin made my night, vain as it might sound.

⛩

A couple of weeks after Renee left Tokyo, I took a business trip to Hungary; a journey which almost didn't happen. Japan had been dealing with swine flu for nearly a month and many companies had banned international travel during that timeframe. The Japanese government was doing everything it could to prevent the pig flu from infecting its citizens, though it didn't quite succeed as more than 400 people were diagnosed, but the epidemic had gradually slowed down. I hadn't seen or heard about a country that was more paranoid about health issues than Japan.

"You're lucky you missed the whole pig flu thing," I started our conversation when Renee Skyped me after I returned to Tokyo from Budapest.

"I'm glad I got out because I needed to be home but I heard the government's restricting travel for its citizens abroad because they're afraid more people would catch it or spread it while overseas."

"Yeah, my business trip to Barcelona, one of my favorite cities in the world, was cancelled. I wasn't happy."

"As a nurse I have to tell you far more people would catch the regular flu and die from it than the bacon flu."

"Don't tell me, tell Prime Minister Asshole, I meant Aso. It's getting kind of nutty because the pig flu is on the news every five minutes and is described in such an ominous way as if it was the black plague that was going to wipe out a nation of 125 million. Surgical masks are flying off the shelves in stores. Some people have taken advantage of the crisis and have been selling the masks online for triple the usual price."

It goes without fail that one person's crisis is another's business opportunity. It reminded me of the time when a major hurricane hit the East Coast in the U.S., where some gas stations jacked up the price of oil to $5.00 a gallon from about half that amount. Outrageous! Opportunists abound regardless where you might be in the world.

"The media always sensationalizes everything as they usually do elsewhere but it seems the pesky virus has truly disrupted many people in business and created a big scare," Renee said.

"It definitely has. About half the people in my office wore a mask and the place looked more like a makeshift hospital. During my Japanese lessons, Miyagi Sensei taught me a bunch of words related to the pig flu and strongly advised me to wear a mask."

"That's very Japanese of her. At least she showed up for work."

"It's business as usual. You come to work unless you have to be hospitalized. It's the Japanese spirit. She also recommended a hospital for me to go to in case I get infected, and what proper precautions to take. She seemed genuinely concerned for my well-being."

"Wow, that's very nice, coming from a language teacher you barely know."

After Hungary and amidst the swine-flu insanity, I managed to go to Michigan in the American Midwest to attend a friend's wedding in mid-summer. When I returned to Tokyo Narita Airport from attending Roberts's wedding in Kalamazoo, we sat in the plane for an extra 30 minutes. Half a dozen people in space suits, goggles, and impermeable masks came on board with their temperature cameras scanning for possible victims and passing out forms to fill out.

It was a well-orchestrated safety precaution and looked like a scene straight from the *X-Files*. It was a bit of a hassle but I understood and appreciated the precaution. I was more impressed that two days after I'd returned to Japan, a government official called me and asked me if I was in good health or if I'd come down with the swine flu. At least that was what I could decipher and conclude from the phone conversation since the man only spoke Japanese and I understood maybe half of it.

The man repeated the word *infuruenza* (flu) a few times and I kept saying, "*kakatte nai desu* (I'm not suffering from it) and *daijōbu desu* (I'm fine) and *arigatō gozaimasu.*" They were very thorough and I imagined they'd called every passenger, as much as they could, who'd traveled abroad and returned to Japan during the epidemic to ensure they contained the flu. I'm not sure if the American government would have done the same but it was the right thing to do.

Episode 17 (Jūnana): The Aikido Kid

I heard about aikido when I watched my first Steven Seagal movie some 15 to 20 years ago. Seagal was one badass aikido master and one of the highest-ranked aikido practitioners in the world at some point. He had a seventh-degree black belt and learned it while living in Japan as a young man. While it was a bit late for me to become an internationally acclaimed actor skilled in the Japanese martial art, I did really like the philosophy and the smooth movements associated with aikido. I learned from surfing the company intranet one day that there was a company-sponsored aikido club. Having nothing to lose, I emailed the contact person, in English, hoping that someone would respond to provide info and how to join. My only hesitation was whether I would understand the instructions. Not understanding the tree pose in yoga was one thing, becoming a punching bag, even if inadvertently during a martial art practice, was something else. The response came a day later.

"Chen-san, this is Hiro Tateno. I am an instructor here. You are very welcome to join. We practice three times a week, on Mondays, Wednesdays, and Fridays, in the OTC building near Ningyōchō. Please come any time and ask for Hiro."

That was easy. Japanese lessons wouldn't be complete without some cultural activities to round them out. The master plan was being executed as I'd hoped for. From a quick chat with Murayama-san, I learn that the *dōjō* (practice hall) was just a couple of subway stops from where I worked in Nihonbashi. I emailed Hiro back and said that I would meet them on Friday.

"Very good, Chen-san. We will have Master Suzuki from the world headquarters as instructor on Friday. It is very important because we will have *nomikai* after the practice," Hiro responded in perfectly written English.

I arrived at the *dōjō* with much anticipation one Friday evening and knew immediately when I saw Hiro. Known to the other club members as Tateno Sensei, Hiro was a fourth-degree black belt who had retired from the company a few years ago and was practicing five times a week at different *dōjōs* across Tokyo.

"Welcome, Marcus. Have fun and I will translate everything for you. Don't worry, be happy." The man greeted me with a firm handshake and a big smile. I liked his easy-going manner right way. "First, let me explain the meaning. Aikido means the way of harmonizing the 'chi' (energy). It is a very different kind of martial art both in philosophy and form because its movements are all defensive. Different from other Japanese martial arts such as karate or jujitsu, the goal for aikido is never to attack and hurt an opponent," Hiro explained very slowly and clearly. He then paused to give me a chance to ask questions.

"So, it's kind of like tai chi, where we should try only to deflect and neutralize the opponents when attacked?"

Having learned tai chi in the past, I saw the similarities where you pivot and spin to shift an opponent's movements and energy, using it against him, but only to control and stop the attack, not to harm.

"That's right. In aikido we use a mixture of grappling techniques to throw an attacker to the ground and pin them down. There is no competition in aikido, only demonstrations for the public."

It didn't take long to feel comfortable around Hiro with his relaxing demeanor, good sense of humor, and enthusiasm about aikido. Most importantly I understood everything he was saying. He assured me that there was nothing to worry about and that he would practice with me throughout my first aikido lesson. He also insisted I call him Hiro, his first name and a very common one in Japan. This is a gesture that isn't common in Japan, especially when someone is considerably more senior or older. I, however, obliged.

"Now come with me to help set up the *dōjō*." Hiro gestured for me to follow him to a large meeting room with a big pile of large, jigsaw puzzle-like rubber mats in various colors.

"Is this where we do the wax-on-wax-off exercise?" I was alluding to the classic '80s movie *The Karate Kid*. To his credit, he got the reference right away.

"Ah, no Mr. Migayi here I'm afraid. Everything is happening for real and we practice with real people right away."

We, along with a dozen others, quickly converted the large meeting space into a makeshift *dōjō* by pushing the office tables and chairs to the side and placing these large, interlocking rubber mats in a big rectangle to provide cushion. Someone had placed a large, framed picture of aikido founder, Grandmaster Ueshiba Sensei, on a chair and voilà, the company aikido *dōjō*.

Minutes later a dozen more people entered the *dōjō*, first by bowing to the picture of the Grandmaster and then sat in a *seiza* position (a traditional and formal form of sitting in Japan) and then bowed again. Next the sensei from the worldwide aikido headquarters came into the room and bowed to the picture of the grandmaster, turned around, bowed to everyone, and then we all bowed back to him with foreheads touching the mat.

Did I mention that there's a lot of bowing in Japan?

This fellow, Suzuki Sensei, a sixth-degree black belt, was built like Popeye. One look at him and I knew that he could inflict maximum damage if you decided to mess with him. Hiro introduced me to the 20 or so practitioners in a short speech but I understood only about 30 percent of it. I looked around and realized that I was easily the second youngest person in that room except for a French lady who seemed somewhat out of place.

"We will start by stretching hands and wrists and legs, and then practice the *ukemi*. This means falling on your butt or falling and rolling forward using the elbow as support when hitting the floor."

The practice began officially with a "volunteer" for Suzuki Sensei to demonstrate the key lessons of the evening. Hiro explained patiently, step by step, as I took it all in.

This illustration was done by someone, usually a black belt, simulating a fist strike or hand chop toward the defender (Suzuki Sensei). Suzuki-san then immediately deflected, grappled, turned, and pinned the attacker on the ground, all in about three seconds. Throughout the demonstrations, the attacker's face consistently showed grimaces of agony and his one free hand tapped the mat signaling surrender (and pain). This didn't look like fun but it was too late to back out; time to man up.

"Now it is our turn to practice that move. Suzuki Sensei will walk around to help with correcting everyone's form. We will start each practice move by first bowing to our partner and say '*onegaishimasu*.' We will then repeat the word and bow again after sparring with a partner."

This word *onegaishimasu* has many meanings, one of which is 'please.' Please be gentle and don't break my arm or sprain my wrist; very fitting.

And so, this was how we practiced for 30-40 minutes, where I was definitely harmonizing my face with the floor frequently but not my *chi* or anything else. I constantly kissed the rubber mat during the session and spent more time falling and tumbling than standing up. Every few seconds I heard a thud or a thump as someone flew in the air, doing a half-somersault and some other graceful form as they landed on the mat with their faces down. It wasn't what I'd envisioned but then there was a first time for everything. I didn't understand much of what Suzuki-san said, but Hiro was kind enough to simplify and told me just to practice falling down which is critical to avoid injuries.

As I spent more time on the floor and getting up more slowly as the evening went on, Hiro instructed me.

"Now stand up. When I move, you move."

"Just like that?" I got up from the floor, half cracking up.

"Yes, just like that. Now when I move, you move." He repeated.

"Just like that? Hell yeah!" I jerked my head hard right.

"Yes, but wait for me to strike first, OK?" My sensei and new friend now seemed a bit confused.

"Hey, Hiro, you like hip hop?" I asked, having worked out the night before in the gym to a song by rapper Ludacris called "Stand Up" where the phrase "When I move, you move" is repeated many times in its lyric.

"Yeah, I know hip hop but aikido is better."

I wasn't sure if Hiro knew I was messing with him but I had a feeling I was going to like this guy a lot. For the rest of that first session, I kept playing that Ludacris song in my head and it helped me to relax.

"How long would it take me to get a black belt?" I asked.

"Well it depends on the person, but it can be three years, five years, or more. You must attend at least 30 practice sessions to be eligible to take an exam then you have to pass to become an official aikido practitioner."

They took that seriously. Five levels to black belt, each with an increasing number of required practices and a live exam in front of judges. Fair enough. I was sure that in two to three years I would make some sense of what was happening and that I might be lucky enough to earn a first-degree black belt in about ten years.

The *nomikai* that took place afterwards was fun, and to me, the reward. I was glad to have some nourishment after those new bruises that were forming rapidly on my wrists, arms, shoulders, and my bum. Hiro, a true gentleman who rode an impressive vintage BMW motorcycle at least twice his bodyweight to the *dōjō*, rolled his bike and led the group (including Popeye) on foot to a nearby *sushiya* (sushi restaurant) where these guys were regulars.

Mugs and mugs of draft beer appeared in front of us in lightning speed and Hiro raised a glass and said, "*Otsukaresama deshita!*"

After a few drinks, people started to feel more relaxed and braver and a few individuals peppered me with questions. Amazingly they all spoke decent English, enough for me to understand the questions. I also busted out some textbook *Nihongo* I picked up from my lessons and explained how it was a pleasure and an honor to learn a Japanese martial art while living there and that I looked forward to practicing with them. I'd survived my first aikido lesson unscathed and thoroughly enjoyed the social aspects with my new club.

Episode 18 (Jūhachi): Elegant Violence

"So how's the aikido thing going? You still enjoyed getting slammed to the floor?"

I caught up with Joe for lunch one day after we both got back to Tokyo from our travels.

"You gotta start somewhere, just like our careers. Crawl before we walk. It's therapeutic for me."

"Haha, you're too Zen for me. That sounds like pain. I'd rather get my cultural experiences in the *izakaya* and practice Japanese with the girls. Anybody hot there?" A predictable comment coming from Joe, the single guy.

"Dude, you're too funny. There's a French chick. I think her boyfriend is Japanese. She's too young and pretty to be hanging out with all the grandpas there. I'm pretty sure she's like 30 or something."

"Perfect age for me. Listen, since we're talking martial arts, I'm going to see a sumo match. Wanna join us?" Joe pivoted to a related topic and away from my self-inflicted torture.

"D'you like seeing huge fat men wearing nothing but a jumbo diaper standing on a small dirt ring trying to shove each other outside of the tiny circle?" I wasn't so sure I needed to pay money for that.

"Oh, come on, it's the national sport and everyone's talking about this big tournament. You would like it because it's a martial art. We'll have a few beers there and then we hit the *izakaya*."

I did some research and became more interested in going after learning a bit of history about sumo. The tradition dates back at least a millennium, apparently created for the enjoyment of the ruling lords or the imperial court and for samurais needing an alternate income. Well, at least the people in power in Japan didn't try to put them in a ring to duel with wild beasts and see if they would survive as they did in Rome. The word sumo sounds much better in Japanese and it literally means "jumping on each other." Looking at historical records, the appearance of these sumo wrestlers hasn't changed much through the centuries. These are super-sized men with extra body fat (but extremely strong) wearing an enormous, skimpy loin cloth that barely covers their private parts. They have the same hairstyle, which is very long hair that's pinned into a topknot on their crown. Six divisions of sumo include about 700 professional wrestlers, and many at the top division, the *makuuchi*, were foreigners at that time (mostly Mongolian, with some Russian, Georgian, Chinese, Korean, and even a Bulgarian.)

"I thought all the wrestlers were Japanese?" Joe observed when I later told him what I'd learned.

"Me too. I guess it's part of globalization. They all have names in kanji, and what cool names."

"Can you read the kanji?" Joe asked, sounding surprised.

"Is there sand in the desert? Of course. Mandarin's my mother tongue, remember?"

"Right, you're the man who speaks eight languages."

"Well I've studied eight. So, the two *yokozuna* (grand champions), who are both Mongolian, are called Asashōryū, which means 'The Morning Blue Dragon,' and Hakuhō, which means 'White Crane.'"

"That's awesome. I want to have a sumo name too. Joe is just too generic."

"The judges or referees also wear a cool costume; probably hasn't changed for centuries."

"Yeah, I like the elaborate robe and the funny black hat and their fan."

The matches were preceded by the "summoner" calling in the titans, who waited by the ring, by "singing" their names and inviting them to the *dohyō* (the ring). Both men entered spraying salt onto the dirt ground to purify the ring and slapped themselves on the face, shoulders, and elsewhere to get pumped up and ready for battle. After a few more ritual moves such as squatting down in a wide stance and lifting and stomping each foot, the fighters stood still for just a few seconds to set their feet.

The matches commenced when both men received a signal from the referee and each jumped up from the crouched position at the same time. Most bouts only lasted for a few seconds when one pushed the other outside the ring, or forced the opponent to touch the ground with anything other than the soles of his feet. I must have watched 20 matches throughout the afternoon but time just flew as I was captivated by this unique and fascinating sport. I have to admit that it was an experience like no other and I became a fan instantly after witnessing the strength and skills that these giants possessed. It was violent yet elegant.

Thousands, perhaps tens of thousands, packed the National Martial Arts Center to watch these national matches which only happened a few times a year. Most spectators were men but women occasionally attended but are in the minority. The closest thing to a Western sport that I can think of is Greco/Roman style wrestling where participants attempt to pin the opponent to the floor. But the skillset of these gentle giants was very different and the atmosphere was relaxing and highly respectful. One distinction was the short ceremonies or rituals performed in between matches. The sport and the sumo wrestlers were so revered that right before each bout starts, there was stunning silence in this massive arena. Thunderous claps usually followed the end of each match to give approval and appreciation to their talented maneuvers.

VIPs in the boxed seats up front were served light meals and drinks. Others like me who didn't want to shell out a couple of hundred dollars sat in bench seats and made occasional runs to the concession stand to grab a cup of beer and a bento box with sushi.

One thing I like about sumo, which is considered a martial art, is that no one seems to get hurt, at least in the ring. This is very unlike its distant cousin, boxing, where visible blows and physical damage are often apparent immediately and sometimes after the competition.

After watching the clash of the titans for a few hours, I was famished. Fittingly Joe, I, and our Japanese friends went to a nearby restaurant to have the superfood for sumo wrestlers, the *chanko nabe* (special hot pot for sumo). Inspired by the colossal warriors, we ate like savages, devouring massive quantities of chicken, beef, tofu, fish, and lots of vegetables in the largest clay hot pot I'd ever seen in my life. It was the perfect ending to a day focused on the venerable Japanese sport.

Episode 19 (Jūkyū): The Fuji (Prelude)

'Those who dare to fight deserve praise even if they fail, for they shall never be with those cold and timid souls who know neither victory nor defeat.' — Teddy Roosevelt.

It was the best of times, it was the worst of times. It was the most brilliant thing I did, it was the most idiotic action I took. Ascending Mt. Fuji was a tour de force and a paradox in many ways. It was a complete failure and utter disaster in every aspect. It was also a tremendous accomplishment and an absolute triumph in every regard.

Six weeks before, in Michigan, U.S.A

"D'you plan to climb Mt. Fuji while living in Japan?" Big Nate asked me out of the blue while we huddled around the kitchen one evening in the lakeside cabin where eight of us business-school friends were staying while attending Roberts's wedding.

"I can see it from the comfort of my bedroom in Tokyo. So, no, I do not."

"Ah, you see, you can't really say that you've lived in Japan if you don't experience the hike to the top of Mt. Fuji. You need to do it," Big Nate said, trying to get a rise out of me.

"Sounds like a challenge. It's not that I *won't* do it; I just haven't thought of it. I mean, why would I?"

"Don't be a wuss; you need to do this," Big Nate said. "I'll personally go to Tokyo to make sure you do this thing so you don't regret it for the rest of your life."

"OK, you're on. Who else wants to do the Fuji?" I accepted the challenge and looked around the room for more climbers and would-be visitors to my new home.

Unbeknownst to me at the time, Big Nate thought he was about to be out of a job and was looking for a place to hang out for a while (the sneaky bastard!)

The guy is about two meters tall and built like an NFL linebacker, was a semi-professional race car driver who used to spend days at a time without food and water in the smoldering heat in the Mojave and Baja deserts to test (while trying to destroy) the cars he piloted. I simply thought he needed to burn off some calories and show off his manliness. Why else would he fly across half the globe to climb a mountain that's not really all that tall.

"I must crash this party. I'd like to partake in the summit to Mt. Fuji." Steve wasted no time to announce that he was in.

Steve, who grew up in South Central L.A. and was an amateur firefighter, spent four years in Baghdad dodging IEDs (improvised explosive devices), suicide bombers, and sniper fire, and came home triumphantly without a scratch. The Fuji climb sounded like a leisurely hike to him.

"Dude, I'm in it, to win it." Erik, never one who liked to be left out of a good time, made an impulse decision to join the expedition.

Erik, who claimed to have the biggest biceps on campus (a title that our classmate Vladimir vehemently disputed), ran with one-ton bulls in Pamplona, Spain, with a bright red headband, just asking to be gored. Unsatisfied with that experience, he then scuba-dived with great white sharks twice his size in the South Pacific without a guide.

He'd gone to the edge and this didn't seem remotely challenging to him.

"Any more takers? The more the merrier and *mi mansion es tu mansion*," I inquired after I gladly offered up my place to accommodate anyone who would make the long journey to Tokyo.

After a bit of silence, more people spoke up.

"Hmmm, that's tempting. July's tough as I'm trying to close an important deal I've been working on." Mike, the former Navy officer who saw combat in the former Yugoslavia in the 90s and captain of our rugby team in business school who turned into a serial entrepreneur, threatened to join the mission but had to abort to tend to a more important matter.

"Man, really too bad because I have to be with clients in Israel, Jordan, Columbia, and Chile the first half of July." Another Erik, who hails from Cleveland and is a former Bay Watch actor turned venture capitalist extraordinaire, showed great enthusiasm for the excursion but couldn't pack it into his jet-set calendar.

Fast Freddy, Vladimir, and Roberts all sported a pensive look throughout the discussion but decided to pass on the opportunity. So in the end, there was the gang of four who committed to this journey to the top of Fuji.

We were all classmates in business school and are part of a greater, life-long brotherhood called the Main Gang. Climbing the highest peak in Japan seemed like a marvelous idea at the time. An ambitious, fun, once-in-a-lifetime kind of deal. Why not take advantage of having one of us already living in Tokyo and in a bachelor's pad (for the time being)? What was the worst that could happen? The Fuji would be a walk in the park.

We couldn't have been more wrong and naïve.

Here's a quick list of stats related to my participation in this insane journey to the top of the dormant volcano:

- Amount of water consumed: four gallons
- Amount of calorie intake: not enough
- Total calories burned: 15,000

- Amount of rest from base camp to summit: two 30-minute breaks
- Change in waist size: ↓2.5 centimeters
- Change in body weight: ↓5kg
- Change in body fat: ↓ by 5%
- Change in muscle mass: ↑ increase by 5%
- Abnormality in lactic acid output: ↑ by 500%
- Average heartbeat per minute: 120
- Probability of permanent heart tissue damage: 100%
- Probability of climbing Fuji again: 0%

The upside of this whole deal, now that it's over, was that most other athletic events now seem easy when we look back to this crazy trip and the adversity we faced and overcame.

Marathon? Piece of cake.

Triathlon? No problem.

Who needs the South Beach diet or Insanity workout program to get in shape when you have the Fuji?

Who needs Tony Robbins to get motivated when you have experienced and conquered the Fuji?

The memories (and near nightmares) and lessons are forever etched in our minds. This most recognizable symbol of Japan that we call Fuji-san, is a majestic, beautiful mountain; so elegant, alluring, and breathtaking, yet so temperamental, treacherous, and unforgiving at the same time. We were excellent friends before the trip, but after the near-death experience climbing Fuji, we became life-long blood brothers.

Episode 20 (Nijū): The Fuji (Part I)

I t was the longest night of my life.

Big Nate had flown in from California and Steve had come all the way from the beach of Copacabana from Rio de Janeiro one day before the ascent. At 3:30 p.m. on a Thursday, Big Nate, Steve, and I went over to Shinjuku Station, the busiest train station in Japan, to rendezvous and pick up Erik who was arriving from New York City. Erik was coming from Narita Airport and taking the Narita Express train that would drop him off at our meeting point in Shinjuku. The only problem was, Erik didn't show up on the platform where the train would stop at the expected time.

We waited, and waited, and then waited some more. We called his Blackberry many times and couldn't connect. We didn't panic, just had to modify the plan and take a later bus to the mountain. Finally, my Docomo flip phone rang.

"Yo, the eagle has landed! I'm on platform five, where are you?" Erik asked cheerfully, surprised that we didn't show up on platform five with beers in hand waiting for him.

"Man, we're glad you're here. We were worried that you got lost."

"You forgot that I was president of the 'Sushi Club' at Thunderbird. I speak a little Japanese. *Konnichiwa. Arigatō, Hai Sensei.*

Now come over and let's get this party started," Erik said, not a sign of jet lag.

It turned out that Erik, who is a nice guy and can be ultra-charming, managed to convince a young Japanese lady to let him borrow her mobile phone to make an emergency phone call as his Blackberry didn't work in Japan. Whatever it takes... We united ten minutes later, bear hugs all around, and we were back on schedule.

We took the bus to Kawaguchiko's fifth station or stage, which is about 2,300 meters above sea level or near the halfway point of Mt. Fuji's summit. I'd chosen this station which connected with the Yoshida Trail. It's the most popular route out of the four possible paths to the summit because it provides a fair amount of challenges and has the average ascent time of five to seven hours; quite doable in one night. The goal for many climbers when going up Fuji, including us, was to climb overnight and arrive at the summit in time for the spectacular sunrise.

We'd loaded up on carbs — power gel, granola bars, rice bowls, noodles, and bread — in Shinjuku and ate more after we got on the bus. We arrived at the fifth station about two and a half hours later, feeling a little anxious, and saw a mere dozen people around the beginning of the trail. All was surprisingly calm before the storm, literally. The trails to summit Fuji are only opened during July and August and I'd expected more climbers from Japan and abroad as this hike up the Fuji had gotten quite popular. For most traditional Japanese people, climbing the Fuji is a spiritual endeavor, one that provides an opportunity to connect with nature, a greater force or spirit, a supreme being. In more recent years, it has become a hugely popular tourist activity for Japanese and foreigners alike. Every year an estimated one-third of the thousands of climbers come from outside Japan.

20:30

Operation Fuji officially kicked off as we commenced the ascent from

Kawaguchiko Station heading to the Yoshida Trail's sixth stage in diamond formation, common in military missions.

"They love us here." Erik said. The man who'd only arrived in Japan a few hours prior from New York City, was now delighted to find himself on the Fuji trail with the three of us. It was already pitch black with a sparse few climbers hanging around and the only light that showed the way was our strapped-on headlamps. After some last-minute preparations and each acquiring a five-foot-long walking stick (which turned out to be a life-saver), we headed in the direction of the summit in total darkness.

Big Nate had brought a backpack for me with a built-in MP3 docking station and loudspeakers on the shoulder straps. We blasted off with some Nine Inch Nails and Guns and Roses to get the blood pumping and set off for the peak. Within five minutes it started to drizzle; within ten it was pouring. Big Nate was in his t-shirt and cargo shorts and appreciated the cool shower as it was still relatively warm.

"Much as I like cooling down, I was hoping it wouldn't rain," Big Nate said. "So, you got any spare rain gear in case I might need it later?"

"No, man. But I think it'll stop. It's just water anyway."

"So, you like it here? I mean living in Japan?" Big Nate switched the subject, trying to distract himself from the downpour.

"That's kind of a loaded question. I do and I don't. There's no short answer," I said.

"We got all night, brother. Judging by your blogs, this Japanese business culture isn't for you?" Big Nate said, referring to my bi-weekly blogs I was sending to friends and family about my experience in Japan.

"I mean, I knew enough about what I was signing up for. Everything we gain in life, we pay a price for it, right? I wanted the expat experience and I got it. I don't fit in here and I miss not having normal conversations with people but at least I'm polishing my skills and knowledge in global marketing and learning to be flexible."

"And you like the life outside of work? You know, the food, the culture here?" Big Nate went on with his line of questioning, ignoring the water from the night sky.

"Love the raw fish, the noodle bowls, the Kobe beef, and everything really. Their fruits are super fresh and sweet, especially strawberries. Love the hip Japanese fashion and its Zen gardens. Can't really get into the high-context society though, drives me nuts. And way too hierarchical. In the end I'm just a city slicker from Texas."

As I continued to share my experience in Japan in the past six to seven months, I realized that Steve and Erik had pulled away from the pack and Big Nate fell back with me since I had a bit of altitude sickness and preferred a steadier, gradual ascent. It would turn out to be quite ironic later on that I, the local guy, had the most difficulty with the altitude and fatigue while my three compatriots who flew in from a world away were on their "daytime" body clock and feeling fresh.

I could see Erik and Steve powering forward fearlessly in search of the sixth stage. I put on my North Face rain shell for my pants and a windbreaker, which turned out to be completely useless.

"What d'you remember the most about Thunderbird?" I asked Big Nate.

"Ah, too many things to count. The Pimp and Whore Party in Scottsdale has to be high on the list. And that trip to the Greek Islands in 2000 with you, Carlos, Gonzalo, and Laurie; unbelievable!"

I had a momentary flashback to one chilly evening in Scottsdale where I wore a *That '70s Show* outfit, sporting a fake Afro, shades with blue lenses, and a big necklace and medallion that weighed about a kilo.

"Funny you said nothing about the intellectual challenge from the classes we had or how brilliant the professors we had that set us up for success in our careers."

"Who cares about that? The degree is just a piece of paper," Big Nate said with a straight face and dose of sarcasm. "We all got good jobs. It's important that we had fun and made good friends while experiencing grad school. What stood out for you in business school?"

"You're damn right about the fun and friendship that came with the process and I wish I'd been more relaxed about it. I have to agree with you that island hopping in Greece was amazing; that entire summer in Geneva in 2000 was one of the best in my life. I would have to say that playing rugby was pretty cool too, especially scoring the first try against those cocky bastards from Arizona State."

Big Nate didn't let the rain bother him, perhaps too proud to admit that it could be an issue. He and I went on to exchange stories of our lives like we never did before, from his love of firearms (the guy owns 30 guns!) to his continuous search for a soulmate. We then realized that we'd lost sight of our wingmen completely.

"Respect the Fuji," Steve had said before his arrival in Japan. He probably did the most homework before we set foot on the dormant volcano. It was his large purchase of mountain climbing gear and the recent report of ten climbing victims in Hokkaido that had prompted me to go out and acquire additional proper equipment — waterproof pants, headlamp, thick socks and gloves — two nights before the trip. It was also Steve who insisted that we get the walking sticks in base camp and it was him who happened to have a spare, dry sweatshirt to lend me at a critical juncture of the climb which in retrospect might have saved my life.

The story of the American climber who went missing and was later found dead off the main trail in the previous month was still fresh in our minds. The ten Japanese climbers who perished in Hokkaido Island in the northernmost part of Japan a week earlier due to poor direction from their guide and inclement weather added an extra layer of concern as the rain gathered strength. We were naïve and a bit reckless in that we didn't do proper training or research about the hike. Most people who climb Fuji join a group that comes with a guide who knows what he/she is doing and is familiar with the terrain and the elements. Or they tag along with someone who's been there or at least is fluent in Japanese. Naturally we did none of the above.

21:30

We had been climbing for an hour and were just past the sixth stage without stopping when we united as a group. A loudspeaker was broadcasting something in English and Japanese. About the only thing I could understand in Japanese was *abunai* (danger). The English version advised climbers to stay on the path and use caution during inclement weather, to not be a hero, and to seek medical attention when you were injured, etc. Fatigue started to creep up for me and air got a little thinner as we reached 2,500 meters. We had caught up with Erik and Steve and everyone was still pumped but breathing a bit more heavily. We started to chant to keep ourselves going.

"Fuji is my bitch!" Big Nate, who was completely soaked by then but remained strong and didn't complain, tried to psych himself up chanting.

"Keep it together, gents! We've got a long way to go." Steve, the quasi-military special ops agent who experienced Iraq knew the potential danger surrounding us and tried to get us to stay focused.

"Use the force, we can do this!" I felt like I had to say something also.

Erik continued at the front of the pack and pushed upward like he was wired on ecstasy (and he very well could have been). No one who just arrived from a 14-hour flight can move like that Energizer bunny without some sort of "supplement."

"How can you be so wired like that Erik? What are you on?" I asked bluntly.

"Dude, I took the two Lunesta sleeping pills you gave me and I slept almost the entire way from New York. You're a genius," Erik explained.

"Holy shit! Those two pills at that dose could have put a small horse to sleep for a few hours. You're supposed to take only one if needed."

My pace slowed and I dropped way back from the foursome. They gave me one of the two two-way radios and my three fellow climbers quickly disappeared into the darkness. For minutes at a time, I was the lone soul on this deserted path and in total silence. The only noise came from the drops falling from the heavens above and my boots crunching on loose volcanic gravel. My upper body was covered in rainwater and the backpack was getting heavier by the second with every drop of rain permeating through the fabric, wetting all the spare shirts I'd brought which I'd forgotten to put in plastic bags. Occasionally I saw a flicker of light or two in the distance above and below me, reminding me that I wasn't alone out there. With a small lamp on my forehead and with the torrential rain, I could only see a few meters in front of me.

22:30

I reached 2,700 meters. Feeling quite exhausted, the thought of quitting first entered my mind. At last I caught up with the others at the seventh stage. No one was bitching yet so I kept silent.

"Guys, I need rain gear to go on," Big Nate said; his first sign of cracking.

"OK, let's go into the rest station here and see if we can find something," I suggested.

"They love us here," Erik said again while he was doing some sort of rain dance with his walking stick and looking down the mountain at the edge of the trail. He appeared to be high on some black-market pharmaceutical from Brazil that Steve had brought, still seemingly unaffected by jet lag.

Lucky for Big Nate we found a plastic cover, a bit small and overpriced but better than nothing. He and Steve both bought one so they could have a better chance against Mother Nature. My spare shirts were now completely soaked in the backpack, a terrible sign, so I wrang out the water while Big Nate and Steve put on the protective layer in a hut that we stopped by. It was cozy, comfy, and warm, and the $10 cup noodles looked inviting and delicious. We were salivating but the mission had to go on. The 30-minute break was much needed, and we grazed on cashews and almonds that I'd prepared for everyone. The innkeeper told us we had at least four more hours to go to the top. Lovely.

Within five minutes Big Nate's massive body frame ripped through the raincoat that was about three sizes too small.

"This is not good," he said as he was swimming again. He appeared concerned but plowed forward nevertheless.

Steve managed better as he is 6' 1" or 1.9 meters. The terrain had morphed into a bit of moonscape with lava rocks in odd shapes and sizes at 30- to 40-degree inclines. We had to go slowly to step on the right spot to pivot, balance, and use our hands at times to stabilize against the slippery rocks.

"Told you we needed the walking sticks," Steve said. "Now let's stay single file and stay focused."

My gloves were also soaked at this point so I removed them. It continued to rain cats and dogs and I couldn't see more than a meter in front of me. A few minutes later, Big Nate, Steve, and Erik were nowhere to be found as the peloton once more pulled away.

Sons of bitches!

No fear, I would just take it easy and meet them at the eighth stage where I'd made a hut reservation for a midnight snack. I baby-stepped for a while and breathed deeply to make sure there was enough oxygen in my lungs.

Uncomfortable? Yes.

Tired? You bet.

Worried? Not really, perhaps too stupid to be concerned.

That would all change soon.

Episode 21 (Nijūichi): The Fuji (Part II)

My heart was at a constant 120 beats per minute and it would last like that for the rest of the night. What made it worse was that the wind speed started to pick up to about 50 kilometers per hour. The climb also got steeper, now at 40 to 50 degrees in some places and only getting worse as we got higher. I lost track of time and tried to break it down by taking one-minute breaks followed by ten-minute climbs.

12:00 a.m.

I reached the eighth stage at around 3,300 meters. I gasped for air at the flat balcony outside a hut. A few other hikers also stopped to inhale some fresh oxygen which you could buy in cans. I found my group who were snacking.

"Thanks a lot for waiting, you rat bastards!" I blurted out, using the little energy I had left.

How was it possible that someone who just arrived in Tokyo from New York City a few hours ago was able to climb with such ferocity and was still wearing a smile on his face? He was surely on crack cocaine!

How could Big Nate, completely drenched in volcanic acid rain and basically naked, manage to stay positive or alive? He was probably too embarrassed to ask for help. He's a devout Mormon, so perhaps God was watching him. I was sure he was crying inside.

And how could Steve, who flew in from 24,000 kilometers away the night before, be able to breathe with ease and actually be chatting up some Japanese lady?

I thought the combination of thin air and jet lag had made him loopy. I also suspected that the guarana powder he'd brought from Brazil and since ingested, was some sort of hallucinogen, besides being loaded with caffeine. I was ashamed to realize at that point that I was the weakest link in the group. I sat down for a minute to meditate and feel human again, then unwillingly got up and trailed the other three powering up to the next hut. There would be three more huts before we get to the Fuji-san Hotel (not really a hotel but more like a glorified hut that served hot meals and drinks) where we had a reservation. I told myself I could do this. I told the group to carry on as I needed an extra minute or two to drag my exhausted body uphill some more.

1:30 a.m.

We arrived at our hut finally and a friendly Japanese gentleman ushered us in for a hot meal. Curry and rice were the perfect nourishment for our fatigued bodies. We inhaled the hot meal in under two minutes like a pack of starving wolves who hadn't seen food for weeks.

"So, anyone want to take a power nap?" I asked, hoping they would agree to it.

"No, man, quite the opposite. We're feeling much better now and we should go on," Erik said.

"Let's go," said the other two.

"That's nuts! You're all nuts! But OK, if you insist. You're the guests," I said reluctantly despite being ready to crash on the *tatami* for a couple of hours.

Looking back, they were right to move forward because we probably wouldn't have woken up in time to make sunrise. At this point I was suffering from severe lack of oxygen, exhaustion, stage one hypothermia, vertigo, mild hallucinations, and wondering why the hell I was there.

Steve generously offered me the only dry garment that any of us had, a North Face fleece. That saved me for the time being. We ventured out into the darkness once more in two by two formation and crawled upward in the unrelenting rain and gusting wind.

2:00 a.m.

I couldn't feel my hands or feet. I was on autopilot and the command center in my brain was no longer able to direct my nerves or muscles effectively to move. My heart was beating so fast and irregularly, I started to think about all the cardiovascular diseases I knew about because of my work and believed I was suffering from one or more of those conditions.

Was I experiencing atrial fibrillation?

Maybe just regular arrhythmia?

I definitely have tachycardia.

Could it be left ventricular hypertrophy?

Did I have an occlusion in the left-ascending coronary artery?

Was my mitral valve malfunctioning?

I had too much pride to quit but I was in seriously bad shape as I had terrible altitude sickness. I was already stressed out from ensuring that all my guests arrived in Japan as planned.

I broke out in panic attacks several times during the night and thought I would go into shock. I stopped every time to take several deep breaths to regain my strength and composure as I didn't think failure was an option. I feared not having lived a full life, no posterity, and to quietly disappear as a result of falling off the track down the mountain would have been horrific for my parents and Renee. I plodded on thinking it would be hugely embarrassing for me, the local guy, not to be able to finish the climb and be carried down the mountain on a stretcher. I wasn't going to let that happen. I knew my thinking was dumb and ill-advised. My mom would have disapproved.

"Fuck! This shit is stupid! God damn it! How did I let them talk me into doing this?" I reverted to my younger self and cursed under my breath for a good minute and I felt a little better.

OK, I didn't really.

I shook off the bad thoughts and sat down to catch my breath and slapped myself a few times on the face, the chest, and the face again. There was no one within 100 meters. What happened to my crew? Did I leave them behind? No, I was going so slowly and they'd deserted me. Sons of bitches!

I radioed the group but there was no response. This was only a test and my friends knew I would come through; they had confidence in me. Little did they know I was on the verge of taking a very, very, long nap.

I searched for guidance and strength. I replayed scenes from *The Band of Brothers*, those brave American soldiers that stormed the beaches of Normandy on D-day with Germany artillery and machine gun fire raining bullets on them. I pictured myself as one of those soldiers and my mission was to take that hill and liberate Fuji no matter what. I *would* do this.

That got me going for another ten minutes. Then I sat down again on a huge rock to avoid a spontaneous myocardial infarction. I took several very deep breaths so that my body knew I hadn't given up, completely running on fumes now. I looked up and realized that I was surrounded by a few fellow soldiers resting on their respective rocks, experiencing the same ordeal.

"*Ganbatte kudasai* (Good luck)!" I said to them as I produced a faint smile to stay positive. I then got up on my feet and drove myself upward for another ten minutes with all the reserves remaining in my body.

2:30 a.m.

I was so close to the summit, I could smell it. I must have gone past 3,600 meters. I couldn't feel my feet and my lungs were collapsing. The freezing rain had leaked through the supposedly waterproof pants and reached every part of my body. The hurricane-like wind was 130 kilometers per hour and the rain didn't quit. Fuji was angry and demanded respect. At this point I was joined by a few groups who were traveling with a guide and were in a straight-line formation with bright lights on their backpacks. I realized that they were a bunch of senior citizens. I was a young, healthy 30-something getting beaten by grannies. Totally unacceptable!

I was humiliated and I tripped and fell a couple of times but got up quickly, paying attention to the edges of the narrow trail. The path had gotten quite steep and slender and a careless step could send me several hundred meters down the vertical slopes and cut my head open if I landed on sharp, hard lava rocks. I stumbled upward for another 15 minutes and could now see the summit. I was once again alone in the dark. My mind said, "Go," but there was no movement. I lay down on the ground and closed my eyes for a couple of minutes and recited Psalm 23: "Though I walk through the valley of the shadow of death, I fear no evil; for You are with me." I didn't want to make the morning news on NHK, CNN, or any news for that matter. My body temperature had dropped dramatically and I had the chills. My head was throbbing and my limbs barely functioning. I was out of food and water. I searched for inspiration and luckily, I found some.

3:30 am

I crossed the red torii gate marking the summit of Fuji at 3,776 meters.

At last I'd achieved the objective. I was elated and at the same time realized that my bladder was about to burst. I relieved myself behind the torii gate and I was sure I would be condemned for life for taking a leak at the sacred site.

"Marcus! Over here!" I looked up and spotted Steve standing tall and quietly in one corner like a Roman sentry shouting out my name. "I'm glad you're alive. I've been standing here for at least 20 minutes."

"Yeah, glad I made it too. I had to fight hard," I said.

"Big Nate may go into shock any second and hypothermia is a definite," Steve said.

"Shit! That's not good. How's Erik?" I asked.

"He's fine. Still a little giddy but he's quieter now."

"And you?" I asked.

"All good. Let's go find them in the teahouse."

We fought through the crowd and united with our other two teammates after a good half hour and downed some hot cups of green tea to restore blood flow to our bodies. We then sat for an hour at the jam-packed teahouse to recuperate. Everyone sat very still and faced down and I wondered how it would be possible for us to have the energy to descend for another four to five hours in the torrential rain and hurricane-like conditions. We were lucky to have found bench seats near a fire pit and we dried our socks, gloves, and slowly we felt that color was coming back to our faces and extremities. We devoured some *udon* (thick wheat flour noodles) with hot soup and ordered more green tea.

"I think I might stay up here at the mountain top for a few days to recover. Maybe I'll serve tea to foreign climbers in exchange for a spare futon," Erik said.

"Hey...you know...favorite place in the world...God..." Big Nate, who'd stripped down to his underpants and went into a slight convulsion, was mumbling something not understandable by anyone. I assumed he was contemplating what he wanted us to do with his body should he succumb to the elements.

With hindsight we were crazy to have climbed without any training or a guide, let alone continuing to climb all night during torrential rain. We were all too ill and exhausted to think about others and Big Nate was too proud to tell us how unwell he was.

Steve was silent, had no expression on his face while staring into space, seemingly having flashbacks about the streets of Baghdad.

I put my head down to thank my lucky stars for getting me through the night. I'd been running on an empty tank for at least two hours and felt fortunate to have avoided a disaster on the treacherous trail.

We met some Americans and Canadians in the tea house. They'd all gone up earlier during the day or the day before to get acclimated to the altitude and get proper rest, calorie intake, and hydration. That would have been the smart thing for us to do. We were such uninformed rookies. We later found out the trail had been closed at the eighth stage around 1 a.m. because of bad weather. We'd barely made it across and were lucky to have gotten to the summit. Much to our disappointment, we realized then that there would be no sunrise to witness, not with that crazy weather.

6:00 a.m.

We were the only ones left in the tea house. There was no shame in admitting fatigue. We'd made it to the top of Fuji and we were proud. We couldn't wait to get to the bottom of the hill but there was just one problem. The conditions were so bad and we were in terrible physical shape but it had to be done; there had to be a way. After a quick huddle and fist bumps, we stormed out of the tea house and fought our way to the trail going down on the other side of the summit. We arrived shortly at the crater. It was barely visible and definitely not accessible. It would have to wait for another time, or not.

The two-hour rest at the tea house was a game changer as we'd gained our second wind. After the typhoon-like weather at the summit, things thankfully calmed down as we descended for about an hour. As if playing a game of peekaboo with us, the sun darted in and out of the clouds the entire morning. Beautiful parts of the valley below started to emerge and we could see shades of the mountain change, ranging from almost black at the very top to an espresso dark brown, a reddish chestnut brown further down, some burned orange in between, and then a large base of green far below, filling out the shapes of this magnificent mountain.

The climb down was infinitely less challenging as the temperature not only got warmer but the rain had stopped and the surface was much easier on our feet as the trails were soft volcanic sand and very forgiving soil. We started to feel our quad muscles burn halfway down the Fuji but we so desperately wanted just to finish, we barely stopped to drink water. We powered down the mountain non-stop until we were back to where we started at base camp and waiting for our bus to head back to Tokyo.

10:30 a.m.

In recognition of completing the unforgettable 14-hour journey, I presented the following awards (redeemed later for drinks of sake) to my fellow climbers:

The Kamikaze Award went to Erik, who went straight from New York City to Tokyo Airport to Shinjuku Station to the fifth stage and up to the summit, taking the lead for most of the night, and down to base camp in one piece.

The Spirit Award went to Steve, who hailed from Copacabana Beach in Rio and traveled the farthest distance (28 hours on the plane), endured his bad knees (from rugby), and completed the obstacle course in third place.

The Most Valiant Award went to Big Nate, who started the climb in a t-shirt and shorts and with no rain gear, and climbed the whole way soaked to his bones and nearly died of hypothermia but managed to fight off the elements to survive and cross the finish line in first place.

The Endurance Award went to myself, who trailed the peloton early in the race mostly due to altitude sickness, with tachycardia most of the way up to the summit, and considered quitting multiple times on the ascent but pushed through to the finish line.

And finally, the Dumb and Dumber Award went to all of us who agreed while we were in Michigan to Big Nate's proposal to climb the Fuji, obviously intoxicated out of our minds and disoriented at the time after drinking Vodka Red Bulls all weekend and operating on two hours of sleep a night.

It was an experience of a lifetime. Be smart and don't do what we did...

Episode 22 (Nijūni): Lost in Translation Redux

We took a coach and then the subway and returned to my mansion at half past noon. All of us crashed until I woke them up around 3 p.m. as I'd made plans for the group. I wanted my guests to take advantage of the little time they had in Tokyo so I was trying to execute the action-packed agenda that I made for day two.

First stop was to go down the hill to Jangara *ramen* shop, *Kyūshū*-style *ramen* shop known for its heavy, pork-stock noodle soup with big chunks of fatty pork. Hearty, greasy, *oishī*! Just the kind of remedy you need after suffering from jet lag, exhaustion, and a massive shock to the body after a 14-hour journey to and from the summit of Fuji. I wasn't sure if they enjoyed it but they all ate the big bowl of soup that came with thick slices of tender fatty pork, some pickled vegetables, seaweed, and half a hard-boiled egg that had been cooked in the dark pork broth, making the egg turn brown. Topped off with a large serving of fried noodles, we had an irresistible lunch of champions.

Next stop was Asakusa for some culture and souvenir shopping in the oldest part of Tokyo.

"I don't think I can go on," Steve said as we walked toward the metro station. "I need to rest more for the big night out later."

"Me neither. I'm barely out of hypothermia and I'm stiff all over," Big Nate said. "A massage sounds good about now."

"Yeah, massage. I could also use some relaxation," Erik chimed in.

With that I cancelled the sight-seeing and souvenir-shopping excursion to Asakusa as we all decided to build up our stamina for the evening ahead and we wandered off to the alley where we could find a masseuse to help us repair, recuperate, and rejuvenate from the trauma we'd incurred on our bodies. We ended up in a place that was owned and operated by a group of ladies from the Heilonjiang province in China. A bit random but it was inexpensive and convenient since I could communicate with them and give clear instructions in Mandarin.

"Full body session for everyone please. Firmer pressure for Big Nate, easy on the foot/sole massage for Steve," who went on to moan and groan in a mixture of agony and rapture. I gave a few reminders to Erik that this really was the whole package and that there were no extra "services" at that place.

After the one-hour restoration session and feeling quite human again, we went back to my flat where we did some laundry, rested more, and cleaned up.

"What's the dinner plan for the night?" asked Erik.

"Gonpachi, a well-known and very popular *izakaya* in Nishi Azabu that's famous for a couple of things. It was in the movie *Kill Bill* with Uma Thurman and Lucy Liu, directed by Quentin Tarantino. It was also the place where former Japanese Prime Minister Koizumi held a summit with former U.S. President George W. Bush."

"Nice! Especially the first part. Are we gonna see the Crazy 88s?" Erik asked.

"Forget about the crazy whatever, let's hope we see Uma Thurman," Steve mused.

Gonpachi was one of those places that was too cool to be a restaurant. About half of the patrons were foreigners and all the servers spoke English quite well, which suited us perfectly. It was a very large, three-story restaurant with a wide-open atrium that felt like an indoor courtyard, all wood in construction. We got there about seven-ish in a cab. Unfortunately, no Uma Thurman was waving a samurai sword and chopping the limbs and heads off the Crazy 88s, but the lively ambience, fine cuisine, and bottles of sake made this dinner a special one for the band of four from Thunderbird. We bid farewell to Gonpachi, feeling exhausted from the effects of Fuji, and walked outside and right into the famous Nishi Azabu intersection which seemed just to be waking up to the night with taxis and pedestrians packing the streets. I did a time check; it was barely 10 p.m.

"They love us here," Erik said. "Where to next, Sensei?"

"I thought a quick beer at Heartland up the street before we go to a lounge I have in mind," I replied.

"And what's special about this place?" Steve asked.

"Well, Heartland is a bar once touted to be the number one pickup joint in Tokyo for foreigners. The claim to fame probably came from the time when Lehman Brothers occupied floors of office space next door in the Roppongi Hills Tower and were regular patrons," I explained.

"OK cool, that sounds like my speed," Steve said.

We walked into the place and had a compulsory beer, also called Heartland (a brewery owned by Kirin), assessed the scene that could only be described as "dead," and left after we agreed it didn't meet our expectations. A few jarheads were trying to strike up a conversation with a group of coy Japanese ladies but there was nothing interesting or scandalous.

Our final destination for the evening was Feria, a lounge and nightclub that came to life around midnight or 1 a.m. like most clubs. To kill some time, we migrated over to the nearby Midtown Tower, which was at the time the tallest building in Tokyo. I selected A927, another popular place with *gaijin*, that offered a large selection of adult drinks. The choice drink was mojito and we downed a couple of those except for Big Nate who stuck with Diet Coke on the rocks like a good Mormon boy. We had some chat with a group of folks sitting at the next table seemingly employing the same pre-clubbing strategy, getting boozed up at a lower price.

When midnight came the wise thing for us to have done would have been to walk home. Unfortunately, no one was willing to admit he was too tired or too old to soldier on. And with that we ended up at the very large and congested dance floor in the posh club that was blasting some Euro-techno and where just about everyone was half our age.

"They love us here!" Erik exclaimed as he smiled his big smile then slowly bounced away to have a conversation with a young Japanese lady in a bright floral-pattern kimono who had orange hair. I could see his mouth moving but couldn't hear a thing.

I looked to the left and spotted Big Nate already sporting a pair of white sunglasses with heart-shaped lenses and waving his hands in the air.

Steve appeared to have caught his second wind and was doing some sort of Brazilian jujitsu movement with one drink on each hand, attracting a small crowd that encircled him.

Minutes later we found ourselves at the VIP section and a bottle of Absolut Vodka appeared shortly after on our table. None of us really knew or remembered how it happened but we didn't care.

"This-is-the-greatest-trip-of-my-life!" Erik promptly declared after our first Absolut Vodka and Red Bull.

Many more Vodka Red Bulls and many ¥10,000 bills later, we exited that place and realized that the sun had come out. It was just past 5 a.m. Twenty-four hours prior, we were half-dead at the top of Mt. Fuji brainstorming an escape plan. We walked out of Feria only half-conscious although for an entirely different set of reasons.

For the second time in two days, I neglected to do the smart thing, which was simply to go home and rest. Instead I convinced the group to stay for just a bit longer to visit a must-see site in Tokyo — the Tsukiji fish market. My rationale was quite simple — when would the four of us be in Tokyo together again? Probably never.

Whether you're a fan of sushi or not, this world-famous fish market and the fish auction is quite a sight to experience. We'd just missed the auction but were able to see the bustling market in the early morning hours where hundreds of people had already begun their purchasing process of any imaginable edible sea life. There were creatures that we'd never seen before back home but the one thing everyone was familiar with was the prized tuna and we headed toward the auction place. We saw and touched some of the enormous frozen tunas on the floor, some as long as two meters and each worth tens of thousands of dollars and some up to $100,000. Suddenly hunger struck and what else would you eat for breakfast in Tsukiji? Raw fish obviously. We found a sushi joint and had some of the freshest sushi for breakfast, which I think was the first time for all of us. These dead fish were still swimming in the ocean just a few hours before they met our mouths. It was another incredible cultural experience that I will always remember.

The last day for my honored visitors was a quiet one as I think the lack of sleep and jet lag had taken its toll for them. We took it easy during the day and had another traditional Japanese meal at a nice *izakaya* in Shinjuku. I was able to persuade another classmate from Thunderbird, Hirori, to come out and join us for the *kaiseki* dinner. We enjoyed this very traditional Japanese dinner of eight or ten courses; small plates or quantities, like tapas, served in colorful, lavish lacquerware. That evening it included vegetables and salad, raw and cooked fish, pickled vegetables, tofu, grilled meat, rice, and *soba* noodles.

The grand finale for the weekend was a trip to the 52nd floor of the Park Hyatt Hotel in Shinjuku where they shot the Academy award-winning movie *Lost in Translation*, a film I've watched at least ten times.

Disappointingly neither Scarlet Johansson nor Bill Murray was hanging out at this upscale jazz bar perched up high above the Tokyo metropolis. But it was a perfect way to cap off an eventful journey for my good friends who'd come to visit me from a world away. Nothing scandalous there, just a relaxing evening with good company and a cocktail always in hand while admiring the spectacular view of the magnificent city and wondering what went on in the lives of the 35 million people that populated the nightscape down below.

"Yo, Chen-san, you're living the dream that we all dreamt of," Erik said.

"Ha. It's just a job for a few years, that happens to be in Tokyo." I tried to downplay the whole thing although it had always been part of the master plan.

"Don't be stupid. Most guys would give their left testicle to do what you do. You know, to be an expat, no less in an incredible place like Japan," Nate chimed in.

"Yeah, I guess I'm pretty lucky, considering I was unemployed for a while after business school, and then test-driving cars in the Arizona desert just a few years ago. Life's crazy."

"Dude, you went from delivering drug samples to doctors in L.A. to become a global marketer in Tokyo in a few short years. What's the secret sauce?" Steve asked.

Never comfortable with compliments, I managed to produce an answer with what came to my mind first without thinking much at all. In my twenties while living in L.A. as a sales rep, I caught the acting bug and tried out for many roles in commercials and TV shows.

"Man, you know I'm just a Hollywood reject. I decided to audition for the role of an international marketer, and I finally nailed the role after a few tries, working really hard at it. That's all. I'm just playing the role. It's a job."

"Shut up! You would still be poor if you went for acting," Big Nate said. "I mean we were all poor in school a few years ago but that was an investment for the future. Look at you now! You're at the top of the world, literally."

Steve jumped in. "Hey, man, it's just a job *only* if you think it's just a job. You have the power to write the script on your assignment and shape your job into whatever you want it to be. You will touch and influence more people because you have a global role. Own it, brother."

"And you're making sick money because of the expat package, no?" Erik asked before I had a chance to respond.

"I do OK on pay. But wealth is relative and there's a trade-off for everything, right? We all earn a lot more now than before business school but we also spend a lot more. We also have less time because we feel obligated to work longer hours because of the pay. The important thing is to live in the present moment and enjoy the life we have because who knows what happens tomorrow," I said.

"Well, what d'you plan to do after Japan?" Big Nate asked.

"Hmmm, another expat assignment, in Europe maybe? Or back to the U.S. but at a higher level to lead a marketing team. Haven't thought that far. I know I love the global aspects of the job precisely because I get to work with a diverse group of colleagues and customers and where my reach and influence can be much broader." I was caught off guard.

"OK, you have to give it some thought because if you're not clear on your destination then you won't know how best to drive this thing." Erik gave his dose of wisdom and it dawned on me that I needed an exit strategy from my job in Japan.

"Alright, guys, that's all good but very heavy stuff. Let's talk next reunion in another country. I propose — Kilimanjaro," Steve said out of the blue.

"Only if the same four of us go," Big Nate said.

"They love us there. I'm in it to win it," Erik agreed without hesitation.

I was quiet and non-committal and merely took another sip of my drink, trying to register the scene in the hard drive of my brain. What a truly special occasion to be all together thousands of kilometers away eight years after we'd graduated.

My guests then discovered the fanciest, digitally-controlled toilets that they'd ever seen in their lives and they took turns to take photos in the restroom. I had karaoke in the evening's plan, Bill Murray style, to have a proper ending to this whole weekend production. But at 2 a.m. and with just a few hours of sleep in the previous 48 hours, it was deemed unsuitable for our health if we had to carry on longer. Two sleepless nights was about all our dilapidated and aging bodies could handle and no amount of Red Bull was going to resuscitate us.

We returned to the mansion where Big Nate challenged Erik to a push-up contest for the right to sleep on one of the mattresses. Erik, the man with the biggest biceps (at least in my flat) nearly killed himself huffing and puffing while I moderated the competition. The rest of us were all dying from laughing very hard because we knew the whole time that Big Nate just wanted to see Erik suffer.

The challenges that we encountered and the revelations we received were so engrossing that I dedicated a week to record the trip to the Mt. Fuji summit. I enjoyed the camaraderie and the bond of the brotherhood. I was reminded that the human spirit and willpower can overcome any obstacle and challenge that exists. The good news is that we survived the climb given the circumstances, although I was certain that we all had done permanent damage to our bodies and reduced our life expectancy by at least three years.

I had a feeling we would be talking about that experience for many years to come.

Episode 23 (Nijūsan): Inside Out

After the craziness of summiting Fuji in late July, I lay low for a few weeks and tried to recover from the self-inflicted damage to my body organs. Things got busy at work in the fall as we welcomed some colleagues from other parts of the world to Tokyo in late August. Having lived in Japan for many months by then and living like a local, Ian gave me the task of organizing a global business meeting with over 20 attendees from Europe, North America, and Asia.

"You want me, the *gaijin*, to plan and host the other foreigners?" I asked Ian.

"Sure. You know your way around by now, you can speak enough Japanese, and importantly, you know how to order food and drinks. What else do you need?" Ian said that with all seriousness.

I thought for a few seconds and realized he was right. I was ready to be meeting planner. "What's my budget?" I asked innocently.

"Don't worry about that. Just make sure they have a memorable experience." Music to my ears. It's the best kind of meeting.

I began the tour for our esteemed guests the day before the all-day meeting with a cultural excursion to Asakusa to visit Sensōji, Tokyo's oldest and most spectacular temple that dates back to the seventh century. I explained the history of this part of town and how the metropolis of Tokyo where we stood started out as a little fishing village some 400 years ago. I also described the Nakamise-dori, a street that leads to the sacred temple and a treasure trove of traditional wares such as kimonos and is a great place for them to acquire some inexpensive souvenirs.

"A little jetlag?" I asked the Americans, seeing that they were unusually quiet.

"Not a little, big time," replied Jake, a big guy from Indiana who was built like a lineman in American football. "Woke up at 2 a.m., had a double espresso then a Venti Americano; still not fully awake."

"Haha. Welcome to Japan! What did you guys do all morning?"

"We went to the world-famous Tsukiji fish market."

"Wow, that's awesome. I see you've done your research. You know that's where more than half of the world's tuna are bought and sold. Eat some sushi?" I asked.

"No, not really, not a fan of seafood. Went there for the experience. Huge tunas, some bigger than me. Amazing."

We struggled to carry on a conversation as they were fading fast. It was only 3 p.m.

I did the only sensible thing that we could as a remedy by taking them to an iconic beer hall in Ginza where we said "*kanpai*" (cheers) to some German brews in liter-size mugs. The spectacle and bustle of the high-street shopping district in Ginza got their attention and they slowly came back to life.

That evening I planned a lavish *kaiseki* dinner near the Imperial Palace where we had a private room. It was the first time for many of our guests to experience the traditional, multi-course Japanese dinner where dishes were beautifully arranged and decorated in attractive lacquer or porcelain ware. There was talk of karaoke after hours but I quickly took myself out of the plan, having to help host the meeting the next morning.

There were some casualties the following day as a couple of people went out drinking until the wee hours of the morning and learned the hard way not to mix beer and sake in copious amounts. They managed to stay awake, although everyone knew that they were hurting as evidenced by the beads of sweat forming on their foreheads and the gallons of water they drank. The meeting went without a hitch despite the potential threat of a category 5 typhoon. We were monitoring closely the typhoon that nearly swept through the heart of Tokyo but in the end, it fizzled out and was downgraded to a tropical storm.

The grand finale for our special guests was a dinner party at Gonpachi where we took half of the first-floor space with a group of nearly 50 people. I ordered the highly prized Kobe beef steak the restaurant had available that evening for our guests. Many commented to me afterwards and claimed it was the best steak they'd ever had in their life. That made my day.

"Marcus, are you sure you weren't a tour guide in your previous life? History teacher?" Torkild, a Norwegian colleague based in Munich asked.

"No, why d'you ask?"

"You're acting like you've lived here your whole life, like a proper Tokyo boy who knows where to take visitors, order the right foods and drinks, and you speak the bloody language."

"Thanks. I take that as a compliment, I think. Are you enjoying yourself?" I replied.

"Are you kidding me? The Kobe beef steak alone was worth the trip. Never had a meal like that in this make-believe restaurant. Honestly it's the best trip I've taken in a very long time."

"Wow, I'm so glad to hear. You should come more often," I said to my jolly European colleague from Norway.

"And you're are like a chameleon. You've adapted so well since you moved here. I mean, you were a Jersey Boy who didn't know squat about Japan just a year ago and now you're like Japanese."

"Haha, thank you again. I had to. Plus, I enjoy it a lot, learning a new language and the local culture and figuring things out. It's my fuel," I said.

"You're an amazing host and you're very humble. But listen, if you're not careful, you could really become Japanese," said an American colleague, who made a prediction that nearly came true.

As I planned and executed the week with ease, the whole experience of hosting my former colleagues made me feel that I had truly made Tokyo home. I was most pleased with their enjoyment of the food and seeing some of the attractions in Tokyo. We did accomplish our business goals but that was less important in my mind.

The next morning, I took a trip to Beijing to attend a medical conference. I schmoozed with some local key opinion leaders in the cardiovascular field and discussed how we could collaborate in a clinical trial with some academic centers in China. It was great to see the transformations the Chinese capital had made from the 2008 summer Olympics and to have the chance to practice my Mandarin. Most of Beijing had changed beyond my recognition since I first went there in the early '90s and the pollution was worse than ever. From the Westin in the embassy district where I stayed, I could barely see a kilometer away in the dense smog. Two days in Beijing made me realize that Tokyo had most definitely become home for me and I couldn't wait to go back to Japan where it was much cleaner, better-organized, and with air that I could breathe.

Episode 24 (Nijūyon): Naked Onsen

In Japanese the word *gasshuku* means training camp or what many of us in the U.S. would call a retreat. I was invited to a *gasshuku* late summer with the aikido club to a seaside village where we would practice aikido for two days and eat tons of fresh seafood. On these *gasshuku* trips, people often stayed at a traditional Japanese *ryokan* (inn) with *tatami* beds and an onsite *onsen* (hot springs). It was the same for this retreat, which was a two-hour train ride from Tokyo. The bonus was that the *onsen* for this *ryokan* would be on the edge of a cliff facing the Pacific Ocean.

The destination was a small village called Ajiro located in the Izu Peninsula, famous for its frequent earthquakes and fantastic catches from the sea. It was also the setting for the legendary James Clavell novel, *Shōgun*, the epic story about an English sailor who shipwrecked off the coast of Japan in the 17th century that was later made into a popular TV mini-series in the '80s.

"How was aikido practice?" Renee asked when I Skyped with her to check in.

"Brutal, although some said it was fun. They reminded me that it would take 30 practices for me to reach the lowest rank — fifth level white belt. So basically, I can't even call myself an aikido practitioner because it's only my seventh class."

"You have to pay your dues. It's like anything else in life. Did you think Steven Seagal became an aikido master overnight?"

"I don't want to be Steven Seagal. I'm just having fun. I came for the experience and the seafood."

For 90 minutes, I was in the *dōjō* with 40 other advanced-level black belts who took turns throwing me around and onto the *tatami*. Kobayashi Sensei from the aikido headquarters, a seventh-degree black belt, taught these sessions, which included practitioners from four different sister clubs in Tokyo including ours.

"So, they beat you up good? You got bruises?" Renee asked.

"I was good target practice for them. The *onsen*, the scenery, and the food all more than made up for it."

"What did you eat?"

"Lots of shellfish and different fish in general but I didn't know what everything was. Everything we ate was fresh and had a tail, fins, tentacles, or some sort of underwater propulsion device. The abalone in front of me at dinner was still moving on a plate before they set it on fire."

"Cool! And the drinks? Beer, *nihonshu* (clear rice wine), *shōchū*?"

"All the above. There was enough alcohol for a Japanese naval fleet. I personally had three too many."

It was customary for every person to bring an alcoholic drink of choice and many brought several bottles. I would later confirm that most folks go to a retreat like this one mostly for the drinking, the seafood, and the social aspects of things, and to have a little bit of practice with the martial art.

"Any good stories or scandals?"

"Well, I sat right next to the Master Kabayashi during the dinner party and enjoyed seeing him get abused by his students one by one who came and toasted him for a good two hours during dinner. He was too polite to refuse and he started sweating bullets while his food got cold. His eyes were turning bright red and bulging out. I was very impressed by his composure and his ability to hold his alcohol."

"Sounds like he's not only an aikido master but also a sake master."

"The embarrassing thing for me was, halfway through the feast, everyone took turns to get up to the front of the massive dining room and made a short speech. This is a tradition where people say something to introduce themselves and to express their thoughts and gratitude about the retreat."

"How did you do it?"

"Hiro introduced me quickly in Japanese to those coming from other clubs. When he asked me to speak, I suddenly felt tongue-tied and my legs wobbled from mild stage fright. The only thing I managed to blurt out was, '*Dōzo yoroshiku onegaishimasu*' (Nice to meet you, please be kind to me) and I received thunderous clapping from the crowd."

"Haha. I know that phrase and it's appropriate. It has so many meanings. Very versatile."

"Well after my three-word Oscar-winning speech, I sat back down again on the *tatami* and folks who sat around me were even more enthusiastic about pouring drinks into my empty glass. I was knocked out shortly after I had the red-bean ice cream and stumbled back to the room."

I heard more booze and fresh persimmon were served in another smaller room away from the dinner banquet and that the soiree went on late into the night.

"Tell me about the *onsen*. Don't you have to be butt naked?" Renee asked.

"Yep, strictly no clothing allowed in the bathhouses. It wasn't comfortable for me."

"But the men are separated from the women, no?"

"Yeah, thank God. I don't think I could have done it otherwise. It was bad enough to be surrounded by a bunch of strangers' penises."

Mixed-gender *onsen* do exist in Japan but a bamboo fence separated this one. Hiro had reminded me that the Japanese constitution prohibits clothing of any kind when you enter an *onsen*.

You must strip down completely, wash thoroughly (scrubbing strongly encouraged) before entering the bath.

"Don't they give you towels to cover yourself?"

"They give you this 'modesty' towel, which is about the size of a handkerchief, to cover up certain body parts strategically."

"It's just body organs. You need to get over it," said Renee, a trained nurse who used to have to bath patients on occasion.

"It's not only that there were many exposed male genitals, it was also because there were about 30 of them in a pool the size of a small kitchen."

"That does sound a little crowded."

"Not only a little. And with the water at steaming 41 degrees Celsius, I had to constantly surface my 'little brother' to not get burned and I wasn't thrilled about letting everything hang out."

"When in Japan, do as the Japanese do."

"I don't think the piping hot water is good for my sperm count."

"I don't know; why don't you Google it? I know the minerals in the water are supposed to have healing power."

"I definitely need some healing after the mild trauma I suffered earlier this evening."

"The whole time I was there, I was trying to avoid looking at people below the neck. Inevitably people would get in and out of the water, showing their pecker to everyone else. I started to distract myself, cracking up as a result, by thinking about the *Austin Powers* movie and the many ways he talked about the penis."

Renee laughed.

"I wondered whether the Japanese have also created an extensive list of vocabulary to describe the male sex organ to emulate our rival English words," I continued.

"Sounds like your next piece of homework," Renee said. "I can't imagine you doing naked bathing in the U.S. at all."

"Exactly! Having lived in the U.S. for the vast majority of my life, hanging out in a public bath in the nude isn't something I'd ever done or my idea of having a good time. I suppose the men's locker room in high school after gym class was similar but these folks do it purely as a form of relaxation, leisure, and bonding."

"I guess I have all these things to look forward to," she said.

"Imagine if I said to a guy friend in the U.S., 'Hey, man, you wanna go to the bathhouse this Saturday?' Yet here, not only d'you get invited a lot, most of the time people gladly accept. For the Japanese it's as common as going for a facial or pedicure on a weekend," I told her.

"Did you feel any benefits after all that?"

"Thankfully yes. I can feel the healing power of the rich mineral water after getting some abuse in the *dōjō* earlier this afternoon. And the end of the day was beautiful too. I shifted my focus and thoughts eventually away from other people's genitals and onto the beauty of the sun that was sinking slowly into the Pacific against a lilac and tangerine sky while waiting for others to vacate the pool first."

"I guess I'll have to try it sometime when I'm living there," Renee said. "Though judging by your experience, there are plenty more things I'd like to try first."

"Definitely!" I agreed.

My first *gasshuku* was another rich cultural experience, one that I remember very well to this date.

⛩

"So, you're excited about moving to Tokyo?" I asked Renee a week later. She would relocate to Japan the following week to finish her last year of law school in Tokyo in an American law school that had a campus in Tokyo.

"Yes. Glad to be done with year two of law school and finally coming over there after all these months of getting ready emotionally."

"Well the good news is that I've done the homework to get to know this place pretty well and I can show you what you need to do to get acclimated quickly once you get here."

"True. It really sucked to be here alone this whole time. I don't want to be apart ever again. But I'm glad I don't have to struggle to figure things out once I get there."

The master plan of bringing Renee to Japan nine months after my arrival was being executed beautifully. It was a bit of a strange feeling as I'd lived this pseudo bachelor's life for nearly a year while exploring many aspects of the fascinating culture that Tokyo had to offer.

Life in those nine months was a fabulously fun time, like no other in my life, as I was free to do whatever appealed to me on a whim in this exotic place, not having to worry about money as I did in my 20s while backpacking throughout Europe and Asia. There were discoveries to be made every day, around many corners of that gargantuan city. I was a willing participant, yearning to experience the adrenaline rush of trying some novel food in a new *izakaya* at a different neighborhood, either solo or with friends that I'd made.

Although I was happy that Renee and I would live in the same country again, I wasn't sure how my lifestyle would change as I had no way of knowing if she would like Japan as much as I did and if she would try to get immersed in the culture as much as I had done. Only time would tell.

New Jersey and life in the U.S. were fading into a distant memory and I'd started to ponder the idea of living in Japan longer term. I envisioned a bright future and first-class living for us that would be exponentially better than what I'd imagined were possible before going to Japan.

My second year would turn out to be the year that I began to fully realize and appreciate life's unlimited possibilities. A year that would include a personal tragedy and an important professional setback, both of which would make me rethink my priorities in life. These events would trigger a series of activities that led to me adjusting my mindset and ultimately guided me to rewrite many of my personal and professional goals.

If I could sum up my second year in one sentence, it would be "I was gradually turning Japanese."

My journey continues in *Unexpected Gifts: A Journey to Self-Discovery and Life-Transformation While Living in Japan (The Japan Chronicles ~ Part II)*

Contact the Author

I sincerely thank you for reading this book and hope you enjoyed it. I would be extremely grateful if you could leave a review on Amazon.

I'd love to hear your comments and am happy to answer any questions you may have. Do please get in touch with me by:

Email: marcus@marcus-chen.com
Facebook: www.facebook.com/marcus.chen.58
Instagram: www.instagram.com/marquis.jc
Twitter: www.twitter.com/LeMarcusChen
LinkedIn: www.linkedin.com/in/marcusjchen
Website: www.marcus-chen.com

I look forward to hearing from you.
Marcus

Acknowledgments

I'd like to thank the following individuals:

The Main Gang, my closest group of eight friends from business school, for their friendship, continued support for this memoir and throughout my life's journey: Big Nate C, Fast Freddy C, The Honorable Roberts K, Steve 'Butternut' M, Vladimir 'Biceps' P, Navy Seal Rubes, Erik 'Baywatch' S, Erik 'Wisco Kid' W.

Hiro Tateno and Eric DL for being great friends, mentors, and aikido sensei, and for providing inspiration and guidance on life and career during my stay in Japan. You taught me much more than aikido.

Jerry Chou, a great friend who was there for me on all accounts and enriched my experience in Japan.

Hiro Fukuhara who first conceptualized my Japan expat assignment and was instrumental in making it happen.

My sister, Lisa, who has always been there for me and who encouraged me to finish my memoir.

Shayne Sundholm, a good friend and mentor to whom I'm indebted for giving me a chance many years ago to pursue a career in marketing.

My parents who, by accident or by design, introduced me to many foreign cultures and languages at an early age.

My ex-wife, Renee, who supported me through the Japan experience with great patience and optimism.

Made in the USA
Middletown, DE
24 September 2019